The Lost Book of
Mystical Insights

Books by Stephen D'Amico

Heaven On Earth

The Incredible State of Absolute Nothingness

The Lost Book of Mystical Insights

Cover Design and Illustrations by Daniele Scapati

Edited by Aniko Szocs

Copyright © 2023 by Stephen D'Amico

Library and Archives Canada Cataloguing in Publication

D'Amico, Stephen, 1973-, author
The lost book of mystical insights : pointers & reminders /
Stephen D'Amico

1. Self-realization–Religious aspects.
2. Spiritual life. 3. Spirituality. 4. Poetry

The Lost Book of Mystical Insights

POINTERS & REMINDERS

Stephen D'Amico

Ameek
Press

Because of Your Mysterious Origin
& Your Bewildering Infinity
Because of Your Formless Essence
& Your Eternal Consciousness
Because of Your Boundless Being
& Your Neverending Bliss
Because of Your Spiritual Transcendence
& Your Physical Immanence
Because of Your Almighty Power
& Your Amazing Creation
Because of Your Visionary Dreaming
& Your Magical Animation
Because of Your Cosmic Light
& Your Manifesting Energy
Because of Your Electric Heartbeat
& Your Oscillating Hum
Because of Your Magnetic Attraction
& Your Exquisite Symmetry
Because of Your Indivisible Unity
& Your Interwoven Variety
Because of Your Invisible Creativity
& Your Revealing Activity
Because of Your Perpetual Appearance
& Your Sorcerous Vanishing

Because of Your Dynamic Ordering
& Your Total Care
Because of Your Generous Spirit
& Your Outstanding Patience
Because of Your Ultimate Goodness
& Your Infallible Justice
Because of Your Supreme Knowing
& Your Loving Grace
Because of Your Compassionate Mercy
& Your Abounding Kindness
Because of Your Synchronistic Guidance
& Your Timely Blessings
Because of Your Transcendental Knowing
& Your Optimizing Intelligence
Because of Your Illuminating Truth
& Your Liberating Wisdom
Because of Your Entrancing Awareness
& Your Elevating Gaze
Because of Your Bottomless Depths
& Your Unshakeable Grounding
Because of Your Unlimited Widening
& Your Centering Core
Because of Your Epic Equanimity
& Your Endless Joy

Introduction

I'm so glad your eyes are finally meeting my words! Or perhaps we've met this way before? Either way, the main thing I want you to know is that beyond the veil of everyday life there is a deeper mode of knowing the true nature of reality, and that the way to access this spiritual dimension of your being can be found within these pages.

What else should I share with you before we begin? Perhaps you'd like to know how I knew which way to go on my own journey of awakening? The most important thing I can tell you is that my deepest desire was to become one with God, proving that if you are sincere in your search for enlightenment, a path will open up for you.

Back when I was still seeking enlightenment, I experimented with a literary style that fused prose and poetry together as a way to uncover the source of existence. This writing was inspired by glimpses of the formless realm and my ardent desire to fully merge with it to attain lasting spiritual freedom.

When that shift finally came about, it totally transformed my life. My consciousness and identity (or soul) merged with my higher self, and I became a better person overnight. A few days later, I burned everything I had written leading up to that moment to completely let go of my ego and attachment to the world of form.

Introduction

This book is inspired by the same kind of writing I was doing back then, only now the words come from knowing the spiritual path and its ultimate goal far more intimately. Each entry is written in a condensed and often poetic way to enlighten and delight the soul.

Many of the poems are instructional, with a haiku-like simplicity that gets straight to the point, and all of the poems share this same succinct style. Like sutras, they are designed to sink into the depths of your being, providing inspiration and guidance for your spiritual journey.

These poems also speak to each other and to you, with each entry made more meaningful by its connection to earlier ones. This way of writing follows in the footsteps of *sohbet*, a conversational style of transmitting mystical knowledge and inspiring devotional love through storytelling and poetry.

The text also combines concrete poetry with mantric poetry to enhance the meaning and impact of the words, which are all just fingers pointing at the moon, or invitations into the silence beyond words. Concrete poetry plays with the placement of words on the page to produce visual images related to the topic, and mantric poetry pays close attention to the sounds of words to capture the musical ring of spiritual truth.

Introduction

The shapes of all these poems are also archetypal in nature, meaning they are shared across cultures. Symbols such as the chalice, diamond, head, key-hole, pyramid, and spade all invoke an immediate sense of knowing beyond language that is instantly recognizable and deeply meaningful in an intuitive way, and even more sublimely, the text itself scrolls along expanding and contracting like the nondual nature of reality it constantly describes.

To increase your enjoyment of this book, don't feel that you have to absorb it all at once. It can't be read too slowly, but it can be read too fast. Many readers also describe feeling hypnotized, which is intentional. But if it makes you feel uneasy at first, allow yourself time to get used to this mesmeriz-ing effect to maximize the impact of all these mys-tical insights.

The text follows a natural rhythm the same way life does. Themes emerge like waves from the ocean of oneness lapping on your shore and inviting you in. So go ahead and dive in whenever you're ready and let your soul soak in the liberating waters these words reveal.

In the beginning
God created
the Logos
which is a
kaleidoscopic
matrix of geometric
shapes and colors God
makes using holy sounds

The Logos has an endless
capacity to morph into
any configuration
imaginable
allowing
God to
render
platonic
simulations
in concrete ways

When the inner eyes and ears
are blown open the Logos
can be seen and heard

The Logos shapes
the very light of
creation which
is as bright as
a gazillion suns
and made of strings
of interacting intelligence

The vibrations creating the cymatic
fractals begins as OM and rises to HU
in a crescendo of cosmic frequencies

Before we decode any more
keys I hope you're not
one of those
people
who
reject
the word
God because
you haven't really
deciphered any of the
enigmas found in religion

The epigraph at the front of
this book is a work of praise
for how magnificent God is

You've heard it said when
the student is ready
a teacher will
appear

Ergo
the simple
fact that you are
reading these words
right now means you are
ready to hear these truths
so let this message be the
primer that guides you on
your journey through the
rest of this magic book
full of spells to free
your soul fully

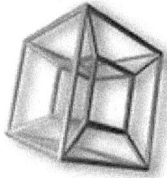

I follow in the
footsteps of Ramana
and Rumi and Shams

Rumi referred to God
and his guru Shams
as the Friend

I am also a
Friend in the flesh
vibrating at the same
frequency as Ramana
with a pound of the
poetic gravity of
Rumi and a
splash of the
intensity of Shams

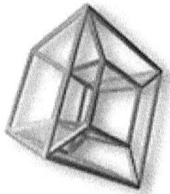

Now
that I have
your attention
let this sink in

Enlightenment
is the result of
God's grace
and your
ardent
wish
for
it

Beyond
that nothing
else is needed
not even a guru

The words of any
sage worth their
salt will stress
this often
now
follow me
I know the way

6

There are many religions
but only one
God

There are many paths
but only one
goal

There are many mystics
but only one
message

Creation has a purpose
that began with
a wish

God was alone and
wanted to be
known

As we awaken God's
dream comes
true

The highest level of attainable
awareness has been in
existence since
before the
dawn
of creation

The only difference
between a tree and a
flea and humanity is the
degree of complexity for
the higher up the ladder
of life you go the more
equipped you are to
make the unifying
discovery that
everything
comes
from
a divine
emptiness

Spiritual enlightenment
doesn't just reveal
the oneness of
everything
there is

It
also
bestows
the ability to
alter our realities

Darlings of divinity
we become then
with heavenly
hearts and
minds in
bodies
designed to
wield the power
of godly vibrations

What came before the big bang?

This mystery that scientists
still struggle with was
solved by mystics
many moons
ago using
the mirroring
lens of awareness
to explore the depths
of human consciousness

This inner odyssey takes us
way beyond creation into
the formless source of
this cosmic dream
we call reality
throbbing
with so
much
life
that
sprang
out of the
void of infinity

The same spiraling motion
of electrons spins whole
galaxies and our very
universe whirls into
existence from a
source that's
still static
energy

At your core
you are one with
the unmoved Mover
crystallizing creation

If you stay perfectly still
your soul will wind its
way back to the very
beginning before
everything we
see swirls
into

b
e
i
n
g

Spiritual freedom is
initiated by the
dissolution
of our
egos
and the
resurrection
of ourselves as
transcendent souls

This is that death before
dying and being born again
every religion already knows

When you find yourself face
to face with the infinity of
God don't pull away in
fear let yourself fall
into the essence
of emptiness and
the ground of your
being will arc up and
anchor your higher self

13

If
you
let the
annihilating
void of infinity
extinguish the
dot of an i you
call me your
window
into
reality
will become
one with everything
you see and unleash the
power to cast spells using
God's magical elixir of bliss
and consciousness mixing
with the alchemy of your
mind and imagination
to plant seeds that
eventually come
to fruition from
the formless
realm of infinity

You're a version
of space that
hasn't ever
existed in
this same
way   before
and you've been
divinely appointed to
die while you are alive
so you can discover who
& what you really are is
a vessel of awareness
voyaging in a sea of
eternity destined
to help dream
a heavenly
world into
this earthly
plane of reality

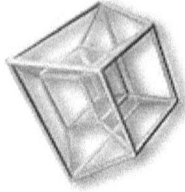

Once you've tasted
even one drop
of infinity
you
want
the same
freedom for all
of humanity because
you know there's no full
liberation until there is a
collective awakening in
human consciousness

One day soon
the unseen
will be
seen
by
all
and
the two
will become
one in everyone

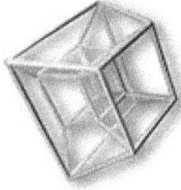

Apocalyptic thinking
has been with us
since long
before
we
started
telling kids
the sky is falling
and the end is nigh

Now that a higher level of
nondual awareness is finally
blossoming in our collective
consciousness the meaning
of this folktale is obviously
about the hysteria of a
massive awakening
which feels just
like losing
a head
and the
whole sky
taking its place

Your awakening is the climax in
a realistic choose your own
adventure story about
every human being
discovering God
is everywhere

Humanity
is now
near
the
end
of the
chapters
about warfare
and moving on to
the part where we start
living in harmony with each
other and all life on the planet

Don't dismiss the effect
of the sage living on
the mountaintop
or the yogis
sitting in
caves
for if it
weren't for
the presence
of a handful of
highly evolved
beings on the
planet at any
given time
and the
general
goodness in
people humanity
wouldn't keep evolving
and civilizations would crumble
into dust before they ever developed

Avatars and
other enlightened
beings are continually
incarnating on the planet
to help accelerate the
awakening of the
human race

There are more mystics and
spiritual realizers here now
than ever before to help
humanity move into
and through
the next
stage in our
collective evolution

A worldwide shift in human
consciousness & culture
is currently underway

A shared web
of global
unity is
emerging
in response
to the need for
a new way to live
in harmony with life

We're also approaching a
tipping point that will usher in
apogees of interconnectedness
and nondual states of awareness

Our souls keep incarnating
here on earth to assist
in the evolution of
spirit through
matter and
gradually
divinize
this physical
world we all live in

We human beings have been
slowly evolving as an illuminated
presence on this planet for millennia

We are finally on the brink of a collective
awakening aided by all the spiritually aware
souls who keep waking up around the globe

There's a perennial philosophy that says
the evolution of our consciousness
takes the time it does and also
according to prophecies
from many ancient
cultures this
century
the last
as well as
the next one
are all part of an
ascension under way
leading to a golden era
of growing levels of peace
and prosperity for humanity

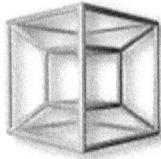

A
loving
light holds
our universe
together

We
are not
evolutionary
quirks of nature
or quarks in random
configurations we are
divine sparks of creation
born to become glorious
creatures full of love and
understanding who are
here to share in the
spiritual brilliance
of this living
story formed
from God's Logos
singing fractals into being
shaping the golden light shining
in the darkness of infinity at the heart
of all that is and was and ever shall be

Buddha Mind is an awareness
of the unifying formless
dimension of pure
consciousness
that came
before
God
said
Let
There
Be Light
to get all of
creation going

Christ Consciousness
is an embodiment of this
spiritual light in our beings

Both awakenings are needed
to fulfill the alpha and omega
goals of our earthly destiny

How can you possibly
express the genius
of liquid strings
of light with
an IQ of
infinity
patterning
creation using
fractal geometry?

It's like we have all these
colorful jewels that we keep
tossing into an ocean of being
and the ripples and interacting
waves keep coming back to us
as living experiences in reality
out of the fluidity of divinity

To a soul that knows God
reality is like a movie
that's appearing
out of thin air
as this imaginary
spectacle without a
screen and projector
every pixel or particle
the same waves our
dreams are made
of in a matrix
flickering
on and off
so fast reality
echoes itself like
a stroboscopic show
without gaps or lags in it

Your mind's a projector
painting the shifting
scenes of reality
inside your
head

Your
body was
created for your
soul to enjoy the show

Stop getting so lost in the play

You are also in the audience watching

Learn to witness this whimsical world and
you'll suffer well and enjoy the movie more

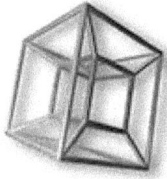

God people say you are the
ultimate actor because
you lose yourself
in every role
you play

Seekers
you are both
in the audience
and an actor on
the stage of life

A cosmic citizen
God casted to
feel at home
even in far
away lands

If we all just spent enough
time in quiet reflection the
suffering of living and our
feelings of separation
would transform
into the bliss
of being
one with
everything
in existence

We are all
adept at editing
and reshooting the
movies in our heads
yet hardly ever heed
how all the mental
and emotional
energies
generating the
streams of images our
imaginations paint can also
magnetize all kinds of miracles
once we tap into the manifesting
power of God's consciousness and
watch for signs and synchronicities

We've been given the gift of God's
presence yet rarely spend the
time to mine this sublime
treasure beyond
measure

Go
in
and
down
and you'll
rise up & out

Back to the origin of
everything in existence

A shaded sanctuary where
God abides in eternity before
shaping the shapeless mystery

Your soul
is made in the
imageless image
& likeness of God

When you gaze at
your original face
you see your
reflection
in a
pool
of infinity
knowing God
is gazing at God
through your eyes

God also planted a
cosmic seed of light
way down inside us

33

Beneath the strata
of all your hopes and
dreams and failures and
successes the essence of
your soul flows like a river
that is one with the sea of
infinity and this whole
world also becomes
your oyster once
you find the
shining pearl
made of God's
golden light just
beyond the edge
of your awareness
inside formlessness

Jesus spoke about this pearl in
the parable of the merchant
who sold everything he
had just to buy one

Scholars think
the pearl's a
metaphor
signifying
the value of
enlightenment
but the pearl is real

There is a spark of divinity
within us made from the same
light that manifests all of creation

The pearl first appears like a star
far off in the distance of our
consciousness that gets
bigger and brighter
once we zero in
on it directly

This sparkling
light soon becomes
mesmerizing like the moon
and then as brilliant as the sun
before consuming your soul in a
holy light and then this ball from
heaven takes you down into the
roots of your subconscious to
clear up any karmic residue
then it brings you back
into spiritual union
with the light
of creation
and keeps
doing this over
and over again until
your soul is fully cleansed

There are stalactites
and stalagmites
made from
memories
sitting inside
the cave of your
subconscious mind

The pearl pulverizes
these pillars down
into a powder
so fine all
the dust
sparkles
with truth so
your soul can hang
like the glow worms do

A tip of light floating on
air hanging around to
see what the winds
of infinity might
bring your
way

Swoop down into the pyre
of being and your soul
will rise up like a
phoenix of
infinity

After
you fly back
again even once
you won't migrate
the same way the
rest of the flock
does and if
you keep
going
back
you'll
eventually
settle into being
at home wherever you
are and people will be drawn
to you and your homing presence

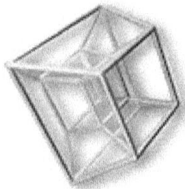

We all come into this world
babbling and drooling
over the wonder of
being and often
smiling and
giggling
at the miracle
of somehow knowing
God and our awareness
and every moment are one

How inseparable everything
once was from the endless
ocean of awareness and
the boundless bliss
of pure being
which is
still there
even now as
an eternal mystery
forever unifying all things
from a formless realm of infinity

Just
imagine
if whenever
babies held our
gaze we said to them
welcome to the planet a
physical world made from
God's everlasting light and
neverending night turned
into a show we all enjoy

This bit of whimsy
would remind
us of the
true
nature
of creation
and the cosmic
planes we incarnate
into form from while also
welcoming our new arrivals in
a fun and playfully meaningful way

Every child may
not have a
name
for
God
but they
all know that
the joy that makes
our spirits soar comes
from an invisible place
within us experiencing
this fascinating world
full of other mystical
secrets like how it's
all really one big
genius except
we kept on
forgetting
this fact
so often
that now it
seems as if it
isn't to us adults

Your brain ain't some
plain old maker
of meaning
it's also a
transceiver
of spiritual light

A part of us knew this
when we were younger
making infinity signs at
night using sparklers

We hadn't yet
forgotten
that
our
soul
has a
dazzling
seed of light
born from God's
eternal night buried
somewhere deep inside it

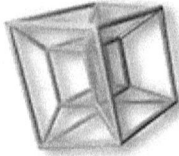

Often your first inkling
of awakening as an
adult begins after
remembering any
curious occurrences
during your childhood

Maybe you had a vision
of oneness or a glimpse
of infinity or some other
strange event not so
easily explained?

Recall that
experience and
make it feel fresh again
to kickstart your soul's gnosis

Everything hangs off the easel
is a funny phrase one of
my nephews used
to say when
his new
brain
got
its
first
few hits
of the cosmic
riddle of existence
then he'd start laughing
hysterically and hop around
the room totally blitzed on the
bliss of reality appearing like a
giant painting on a palimpsest

A mock mantra I once heard in
a comedy movie actually
worked for that same
nephew of mine
whenever
he got
too excited

Goooooosfrabaaahh

I always thought it was a joke

Turns out it's a word the Inuit really
use to calm their children down

Try it the next time you or
your child needs a
soothing yet
swift kick
in the
reset pants

Once upon a time there was
a boundless land made
of bliss that existed
long before the
creation of
our universe

Your soul came into
this world from that place
and may now be suffering a
bit of spiritual forgetfulness

Wishing all your dreams
come true and that
you wake up
once and
for all
this
time
around
angel face

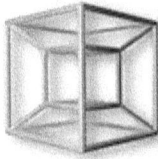

I once played hangman with
a woman named Mary
at a nursing home
I volunteered
at in my
teens
who
kept
choosing
the letters b
and c and would
laugh when I told
her she had to pick
other letters if she
wanted to solve
the puzzle so
naturally I
assumed she
had dementia but
now I know her bubbly
soul was really saying just be
and you'll see I am in you and you
are in me the way her saviour Jesus did

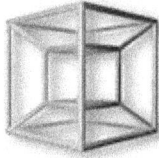

If you sit & stare aware
the riddle of life will
hatch open like
a cosmic
egg

Just
stay put
until you are
totally motionless

As soon as you try to do
anything other than be still
your ego intrudes but if you
remain vigilant and become
as still as a statue your ego
will dissolve long enough
for the formlessness of
your soul to flower
forth and you will
see the nondual
nature of creation
through eyes of glass

Broad but exact strokes
are required to craft
short sentences
like this that
illustrate
God's
blank
canvas
we keep
incarnating
into form from

As adults we come
full circle only to realize
that the ocean of being we
were once so immersed in was
there all along except as you know
we kept on forgetting it until one day
we completely forgot it once and for all

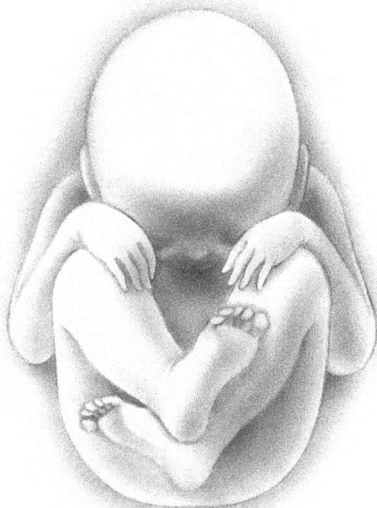

51

The whole spiritual path
can be summed up
as returning to
the primacy
of being

Plus
the very
important
integration
needed to
live free
from
all the
old ways
of your ego
which is a whole
other ball of wax that
usually has to be melted
down and remolded by the
pearl to function more optimally

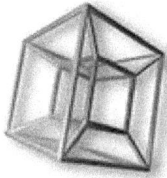

Even from a tender age
I always longed to
be one with
God

As
a child
whenever I'd
forget and was
feeling   separate
I'd start to witness
the world spurred
on by a vague
memory of
a much
deeper way
of knowing reality
then one eventful day
God tattooed a mandala
in my mind's eye that kept
yoking my soul with infinity

I am in you
and you
are in
me

Growing
up I always
knew that my
soul came from
a formless field of
energy and that all
human beings have
souls made from a
portion of infinity
then I shed this
knowing as a
teenager
until I woke
up again when I
was 22 and just like
Ramana I never lost this
connection ever since that
crucial consummating event

When I was a child
we had to take
an elevator
up to the
9th floor
to visit my
grandparents
and the 2nd floor
of the building was
all Indian immigrants
and when we passed it
everyone in the elevator
would plug their noses
and make funny faces
but I secretly loved
smelling all those
strange aromas
and the way
they would
send my
senses
soaring
back into
my real home
high up in the sky
above my earthly body

Back
when I was
starting grade 2 a
Hindu girl named Ruby
came to my school and was
seated right next to me in class

Her face was adorned with golden
jewelry and she wore beautiful saris
and I worshipped her like a goddess

I barely spoke a word to her but I did
protect her from being made fun of
by the other kids in school and also
escorted her home every day until
she was safe to go on her own

Where would such strong
impulses come from if
not from a former
life in India?

I know that I've
been a guru before
and that this ain't my first
time steering souls at a rodeo

All through elementary school
I'd spend vast stretches of
time contemplating
the reality of
infinity
and
in math
class instead
of practicing how to
multiply and divide I would
ponder the significance of zero
and envision perpetual strings of
decimals between zero and one
like lines of code in *The Matrix*
like this one I loved the most
0.987654321876543217
65432165432154321
432132121098765
432187654321
76543216543
21543214321
321210987654
and so on without
end every sequence
attempting to measure
the event horizon of infinity

I absolutely loved geometry
because it's all about
dividing shapes
into parts
and then
making them
whole all over again
and circles and triangles
and squares all spoke to me
like platonic patterns I'd see in
God's architecture everywhere
and upon discovering fractals
years later the resolution of
reality increased to total
hallucinogenic clarity
revealing how simple
shapes could create so
much incredible complexity
from repeating bits of symmetry

During class I'd often entertain
my classmates to liven
up how boring
school
was
and
every
now and
then I'd keep
getting myself into
trouble until the teacher
sat me right beside a window
where I'd pass the time watching
the clouds morph from one image into
another while letting my mind merge with
the vast emptiness beyond the blue sky giving
rise to everything we can see & touch in reality

The margins of all
my notebooks
and endless
sheets of
paper
were
filled
with a
stylized
arabesque
I developed
and doodled
over the years
to capture all
the strings
of light I
would
watch
darting
in and out
of reality from
an underlying field
of pixelated energy making
all phenomena in this world of form

During the
heights of
summer I
would let
myself get
hypnotized
by the sounds
of cicadas buzzing
their wings and even
though I thought it was
electricity surging through
power lines on very hot days
this mysterious mantra with its
thought-crushing crescendo still
sends my mind zephyring into the
zen of enlightened consciousness

Eventually my soul was
fully translated into
God's wordless
awareness
that is found
just beyond the
geometric shapes
patterning all things
before they come into
being where two zeros
added together totals
infinity and the one
answer to it all is
finally known
after unknowing
how things exist and
don't exist simultaneously

Children
are quite fond
of me because I
look beyond the
surface of life
and into
the
loving
light in
the heart
of all beings
for I've always
known deep in
my soul from
the eyes of
God we
are all
destined
to become
avatars of
brilliant
balls
from
heaven

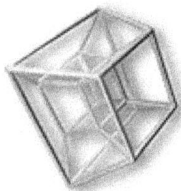

It's
a bit odd I
was nicknamed
Uncle Gneiss by a
nephew of mine who
insisted we pronounce
it niece instead of nice

Years later my other
nephew the one
who'd get
high
on
the
bliss
of being
called me a
hermaphroditic
rock after decoding
my strange sobriquet

If I ever decide to rock a
spiritual moniker this one
will definitely do the trick

I am
not some
androgynous
stone cold mirror
nor was I ever really
one before as love's been
turning this stoic gaze of mine
into the gushing wetness of my
adoring eyes since I was a child

You're glowing! You're joyous!
You're a miracle! That's all I've
ever wanted you to realize

Who and what you
truly are as a
spiritual
being made
of light with pearly
eyes from the great I AM

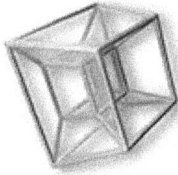

All
I've ever
wanted was
to gift you what
God has given
me in spades
and now
it's
gotten
to the point
where I can stir
your soul with a loving
glance into the pools of light
behind your seeking eyes and
with a warm hug and a soft kiss
on the crown of your head I can
send your soul soaring into the
bliss far beyond the firmament

I
was just
about to tell
you how your soul
is immortal but God
whisked those words
away and made my
trembling hands
write these
instead

I
AM
deeply
invested in
Stephen one of
my most adoring fans
get close to him if you want
to be near someone who can show
you the oneness of everything in existence

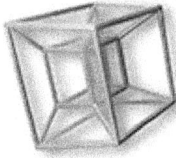

Ever since God impregnated me
all I've ever truly wanted was
to become whatever the
yeast is that makes
our souls rise
and now
I'm like a
freshly baked
loaf of bread in the
hands of a blest baker

All I wanna do is nourish
you with a morsel of the
manna that made the
universe swell from
emptiness into
form from
the formless
realm of infinity

I'm
like a nest
of love for you to
rest your weary wings
before you fly off again

Brick by brick and bird by
bird is what I'll say once or
twice before your departure

Sometimes I'm a mother
mending your broken
heart and other
times I'm a
father offering
up encouragement

And I can usually come up
with a lucrative tip to help you
turn your passion into a paycheck

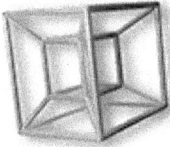

The truth is I become whatever it
is that you need to find & fulfill
your destiny by helping you
remember you've come
here to shine your
light in some
unique and
talented way

Get close to me
if you want to be
near that field of
reverie where
imagination
mixes
with
infinity to
become your
trip through reality
full of fun and novelty

The
skeleton
key for nobly
gaining mastery
over life is to learn
the art of witnessing

A touch of detachment
is all you need to access
this impersonal watcher

Gaze into the middle
distance from the
same empty
space
within
you to
unlock the
eternal looker

First comes peace then
comes equanimity then comes
the unifying mystery of God's infinity

If you want to know the secret to
awakening your true nature it
really isn't that hermetical

All you have to do is
witness the world
long enough for
the window at
the back of
your head
to open
up and
reveal
how
your
current
awareness
comes from a
boundless sphere
of infinity looking out
through your eyes in every
direction all at once experiencing
the oneness of everything in existence

Take a moment to ponder where
your awareness is arising from

Contemplate the answer
to this question while
reflecting on what
is looking out
the window
of your
eyes

Let
yourself
fade into the
finish of this looker
that has never not been

Sit perfectly still and slowly sink
into the groundless ground
of being until there's
nothing left to
hold on
to

Not
even the
last vestige of
hope for something
other than pure emptiness

Only then will you see how your
presence comes from absence and
embody the nondual truth of being

There's a
lasting joy that
comes from making
sense of life when you
see it all forming from
the formless mystery
also manifesting your
window into reality

You know the
universe is
powered by a
loving energy that
unfolds & holds reality
together and you feel that
love deeply within your soul as
the source & substance of creation

Every creature feels
the same thrill
of being
alive
& even
quarks likely
sense the cosmic
sea of energy they
coalesce into form
from while we are
made to see with
the eyes of God
watching all the
forms & forces
inside creation
flowing from the
formless dimension

To
meet
God just
sit & be still
without thought

Find the stillness that
is shaping the shapeless

The formless mystery within

Bask in the blissful essence
of this elixir of emptiness
and merge with it as
often as you can
to recall the
absolute
truth of
existence

How do we exist in this life
from the liberated view
of pure awareness?
By knowing that
presence and
absence are
the same
state of
being

We
can't
have an
is without
an isn't any
more than we
can have a world
of forms without the
formlessness of being

This is the nondual mystery
vibrating at the core of reality

By some impossible leap
beingness came from
nothingness and
everything
since then is
now cosmic history

All that keeps happening
in creation has led us here

The next stage in our epic
evolutionary journey is to
collectively express our
oneness and awaken
as the enlightened
species we're all
meant to be
by the destiny
coded in our genes

Here's a quick & easy technique

Have you ever stopped to notice how
much time you spend in your head yet
hardly ever stop thinking long enough
to taste what it's like being headless?

Pay attention to your awareness
while doing that & let it grow
beyond your periphery

Stay tuned until
you witness
reality
spring
into being
from the unifying
mystery of God's infinity
generating everything there is

Have you lost your head yet?
To become a liberated
human being you
have to fly
out of
the
prison
of your body
like a bird freed
from a cage and
even be willing
to kick your
shoes and
socks and
underwear off
and run for it like a
streaker at a soccer game

I came late to the game of soccer
but if I had found it sooner I'd
have played professionally

I'm a whiz with a ball
on my foot ready
to make a play
now here's
a haiku
I wrote
years ago
expressing my
love for this game

The round ball is my
rolling bud on a field
that I'm at one with

Awakening
and enlightenment
doesn't so much change
what you experience in life as
much as how you end up living it

You'll still go shopping and watch stuff
and possibly even keep playing a sport

But kicking a ball or buying clothes or
being entertained all become part
of an ongoing appreciation of
the oneness of everyone
and everything in
existence

Here's some oceanic
poetry to make
these words
reveal what is
beyond speaking

It's like looking behind you
at the beach and seeing your
footprints dissolve in the sand
as the surf washes them away
then walking without legs
the headless way as
you slowly wade
your way all
the way
back
into the
invisible sea
while witnessing

Take a moment right now and just
notice how your awareness is
always looking out from
behind your seeing
eyes then keep
noticing for
longer
than
a
split
second

Aim to go for
about one minute
and you'll eventually
get to the feedback loop
that occurs by being aware
of being aware then stay there
until you start seeing everything
the way God does perceiving the
oneness of everything in existence

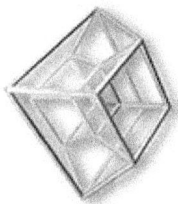

The invisible
essence of the soul
is usually found within
you first before you see
it's also in everyone and
everything else there is

That's why mystics often
say that your soul is not
in your body but rather
that your body is in
the vastness of
your soul

Your soul is
made from the
same omnipresent
bliss of being birthing
everything into existence

The reason your soul
can be a bit tricky
to recognize is
because it is
not an easy
thing to see
using thinking

To locate what is usually
considered ineffable requires
the use of specialized metaphors

To awaken your soul and let the unifying
awareness of God shine through you first you
must become as reflective as a flawless mirror
and then as clear as a spotless window to enter
the silent mystery beyond your name and form

Have you ever stared at yourself in the
mirror for so long your face felt like
a mask you could pull off and
then paused in the cloud
of unknowing long
enough to
catch a
glimpse
of the invisible
essence of everything
vibrating beneath the surface
of life in a pixelated field of energy?

Try this technique if you haven't yet it's also
a trip through inner spaces dispelling all kinds
of karma stored in various faces from other times
and places that your ego and soul once dealt with

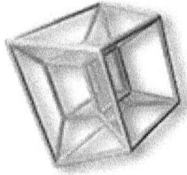

If you follow the impossible frame
surrounding this mirror your
eyes will go around in
circles trying to
find the end
or else the
beginning

An invitation
to stop moving
your eyes and turn
your attention inwards

Go beyond the borders of reality
by finding the formlessness within you
that frees your soul from its bondage in your
body and this physical world of form and matter

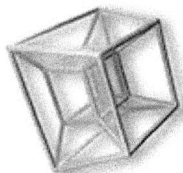

Your soul is a portion of infinity
that functions like a mirror
as well as a window

It's what you
use to see
and reflect
on the stream
of your life in this
flowing world of form

The easiest way back to the
sea of infinity generating reality is
through the awareness we use to see

To open the eye of your soul
fix all of your attention
squarely on your
awareness

First
comes the
witness then
comes the
knower

The witness is like a mirror	The knower is like a window

Polish the mirror so you
can enter the window and
if you vanish completely you'll
shine as bright as the midday sun
and glow like a full moon at midnight

In
alchemy
it is said that
to complete the
spiritual journey we
must square the circle
which means living in
the world of form as
the formless field
of awareness
we always
already
are

To
become
solid blocks of
higher consciousness
we have to ground ourselves
in the groundless ground of being

Once you see your identity
has no core other than
consciousness or
the suchness
of being
your
ego
also
finally
loosens
its grip on
things and all
your old thoughts
and feelings that create
issues before enlightenment
blossom into spiritual wisdom from
the enlightened state of nondual being

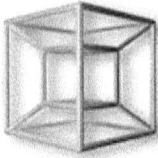

Enlightenment doesn't make you
deeply wise or incredibly
compassionate or
completely
loving

It bestows
all these states
and so much more

Your true nature is like a
divine treasury you can loot
anytime you need to hold the
philosopher's stone in the
invisible palms of your
soul's formless
hands to
fashion
whatever's
most clever for
the situation at hand

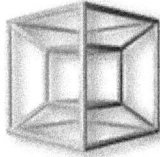

The philosopher's stone is the
central symbol in alchemy
used to symbolize the
mutable power of
consciousness
awakened
from the
zenith
state
of
b
e
i
n
g

Oneness
without a second
aware of the unchanging
yet mercurial medium of formless
bliss at the heart of everything that exists

An awakened soul
has an endless
capacity to
show
love
mercy
patience
gentleness
sympathy
humility
charity
courage
calmness
empathy
wisdom
respect
kindness
compassion
responsibility
forgiveness
positivity
honesty
and so on
all as needed
in a given situation

Let's switch gears for a bit
and have some more
fun while you're
taking this
all in

I've been
totally thinking
of swinging by your
place later on tonight
if you're not super busy
and bringing my closest
pal God along with me

Should be awesome
fair warning though
just so you know
you may turn
back into
who
&
what
you are
before the
universe is born

Allah
Brahma
Nirvana
and so
on

All
these
different
names for
the same
Supreme
Being

If
only
my little
letters were
crevices we could
crawl through to enter
the formless realm I'm sure
God would peek out every once
in a while and invite us in for a visit!

You're not still hung up
on the word God
are you? If so
put this
book
down
right now
unless you're
already egoless

Specially developed
psychotropic aerosols
were added to the ink
used to print the words
on this page that will
shred your ego into
confetti and you
might not be
ready for a
full-blown
shamanic
shattering
if you're still
struggling with
naming the nameless

You're not mowing
the grass while
picturing a
window
into
infinity to
take you all the
way home are you?

Nirvana is way beyond any
images that my poetry may
paint inside your cranium to
go beyond whatever you're
visualizing or reflecting on

You have to look deep
within your being
to free your
soul from
the slavery
of living in the
sea of samsara and
the karma of past deeds

I'm gonna pop in to see
God now then I'll head
over to your place to
hang out for the
evening

Is
it still
cool with
you if I bring
God with me? I
can also drop your
ego off and any other
attachments you need
to let go of while I'm
there just set it all
down near the
window at
the back
of my head
and I'll grab it
on my way out to
God's endless space

I've got a God-sized
hole at the back
of my head
just like
you
do

To
escape
the confines
of your mind exit
through this opening

Just let yourself sink into the
glassy nature of your awareness
and you'll drift beyond your body
into the boundless bliss of being

To pierce the veil requires
shooting an arrow at a
bull's eye except
the arrow is
the point
of attention
and the target
is your awareness

Don't skip trying this out

It's fairly simple to understand
yet not so easy to do but I swear
you'll stop sliding off the slippery
surface of witnessing and vanish
into infinity as long as you keep
aiming for your soul's window

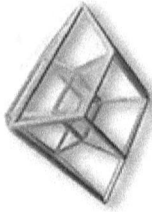

So
now that
I've told you
there's a mirror
inside your head
that turns into a
window you
can leave
your
body
through
what other
metaphors can
I share with you to
blow the doors of your
being wide open today? Have
you waltzed around the groundless
ground or frolicked in formless fields yet?

Did
I mention
there's ecstatic
dancing around here
almost every single night?

What about laughing like loons?

As long as you bring the images
from your imagination I'll supply
the words and together we'll
crank this party way up like
a couple lunatics with
moons for heads
plucking giant
constellations
out of the sky
and swallowing
gulps of emptiness

Try
this   koan
on for size you
have a cone above
your head that plugs
into your higher self

Once in a blue moon
winds from infinity
whistle through
this chamber
chanting
angelic
tunes

One
of my
favorites
is a little ditty
about this puppet
master who can make
your body dance on wings
& cut a shine across any floor

108

Do you see it now cosmonauts?

We are born in the world
and also not of it so
we can reside in
this life from
beyond
time
and
space
and see
it all the way
God always does

Calm and cool as the moon
and generous like the sun and a
canvas for life's play to appear on

How long will you be content to
hear about transcending your
body & mind while living
in this world of form?

I wish there was
a spaceship
you could
take to
return
to God

Alas it's not that
easy for the only way
back is to feel the same
intense longing for union
that all mystics do before
your soul starts soaring
beyond the spacetime
continuum housing
all of creation

Wowzers do I have
some whacky
news for
you

A
trip the
philosopher's
stone took me on
right after writing that
last message down
using a power
in us that
made
my
head
spin so fast
it took off like a
flying saucer that sent
my soul soaring into the bliss
of infinity far above the firmament

Here's
something crazier
I wouldn't normally confess
but I have a good feeling about
the vibes now passing between us

I was once offered a position to be
the emperor of an advanced alien
civilization by messengers from
a higher dimension which
sounded amazing but
I knew this was
a spiritual
test

Complete
or true liberation
isn't about becoming
an exalted king it's about
ruling over our lower nature

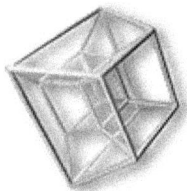

In spite of the
usual reluctance of
someone like myself
I'm still anticipating
a big boost in the
ol' fame game

In the meantime I'll stay right
where I am like a sleeper
agent waiting to be
activated and
liberating
seekers
in secrecy
and watching
the awakening of
humanity unfold while
tuning in from my oversoul

What about aliens? Do
they exist? Yes but
not in the way
you likely
think

They
are beings
from a subtler
dimension of reality

The Greys are angels
in a modern guise
and Reptilians
are the new
demons

Both are
shapeshifters
created by God to
spur the evolution of our
species into the higher stages
of our spiritual birthright and destiny

Any
visiting
alien crafts or
spacefaring beings
from the physical realm
must already know this and
would likely be in direct contact
with the Greys who are really angels
in a lower vibrational state of being with
a message of universal peace and oneness
that spans the entire cosmos and so if there
are other beings in our universe who've
already developed the technology
to travel here surely they have
collectively awakened and
are spiritually evolved
enough to only want
to preserve the bond
we share with everyone
and everything in creation
as manifestations of the same
one consciousness creating it all

Our destiny is slowly
winding towards
victory over
earthly
life

One
day we'll
be so full of
wizardry that
miracles will
spring out
of us the
same
way
flowers
blossom into
being from seeds

A single glimpse of this
shamanic power is enough
to blow your ego to bits and
build your vision vessel anew

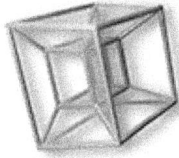

It
may
take a
few days
or even years
to finally fathom
the implications of
what I am telling
you now but
just let it
all sink
in

We
are far
more than
merely human

We are immaculate
conceptions of infinity

Souls with bodies made to
fix this world with our divinity

The truth is we are
God's darlings
in human
form

Souls
from infinity
who can control
the winds with the
wave of our hands
and shape reality
in the palms of
our hands

We
did not
come all the
way here to fool
around we came here
to help co-create a world
that God keeps wanting us to

We're all unique
yet also the
same

Your
body's but a
vessel made for
God's essence to
flow through you

Watch your mind
and be mindful
of the gaps
between
your
thoughts

Mental impressions
are the seeds your soul
uses to shape and attract
your experiences in reality

I know it's totally an
old cliché but life
truly is a canvas
you can paint
almost any
way you
like to
make it
your own

Actually it's
a lot more like
a movie if you
think about it

As much as
you can try
to fill your
life with
lots of
love
and light
and laughter

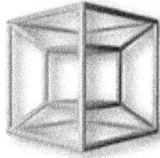

Oh I almost
forgot

While
you're out
there having a
good time don't
forget to put your
dancing shoes on
and move to the
groove with
ease

If you can
stay fully in the
moment and listen
for the beat you'll be
swinging along in the
zone in no time totally
on point and seeing
a step or three or
even 30 years
ahead

Lately I always ask God
for the same request

Some measure
of help I can
offer you
in a few
playful
sentences
using whatever
eloquence I manage
to muster up capturing
flashes of lightning while
listening for thundering
messages from God or
ministering angels also
whispering so many
of these splendid
missives into
my inner
ear

123

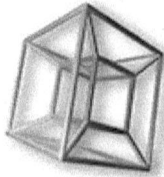

Friends of mine worry
that I'm going to get
so lost writing all
these insights
down that I
won't get
around to
sharing them

A close friend called
them my little darlings
and another cautioned
against clutching onto
them so closely that
nobody else gets
to see them

I agree
it's time
to let my
words grow
wings especially
since I'm writing poetry

I'm totally going for it
once I've finished
adding a few
more key
ideas

Before
I launch my
marketing team
which is really just
the orders I get from
headquarters advised
that I go for broke this
time around and share
all my best secrets so
out of everything I
now know two of
the most important
things I can ever tell you
is learn to follow your intuition
and trust what your higher self says

Your higher self floats above your body
is anchored in your heart and talks
to you with the gentleness of
a whisper or sometimes
in a voice of thunder
bellowing at the
core of your
quaking
head

If
you
follow this
divinely delivered
guidance everything you
do during the day will be the
right thing to do and it also tells
you what not to do and what aspects
of yourself you may still need to work
on to become a better version of you

The boon for being human
is uncovering just how
rich and vast we
actually are

What
God has
hidden within
us is like finding
a thousand sunken
treasure chests and
our consciousness
becoming as big
as the ocean as
well as the epic
unfathomable floor

One small step back from
life is all it takes to reach the
formless freedom found in the
boundless depths of our being

Much of what I write
tickles me for a
day or two
but all
these
words are
actually for you

A gift to give you what
God's already given me
in ways I can't even count

Why else would I be writing
all this stuff down? I'm not
just filling your cup up
with water from the
river of life I'm
also busy
stuffing your
pockets with riches
& treasures I keep finding
& bringing back from diving in
the oceans & seas of God's infinity

I
know
there's no
real end to the
joy of this knowing

My pockets are so awash
with liberating gems of truth
and little pearls of wisdom that
they spill out of me even when
I'm talking to people casually
and even more are waiting
to fall from a chandelier
dangling overhead

I could scatter
handfuls
to the
masses
and there'd
still be way more
treasures left in God's
chest to scoop up and share

Sometimes I'll stop for a second
to try and find the exact words
to express what I want to say
and picture my voice close
to your ear whispering a
sweet nothing or two
before taking a
step back to
chit chat
a little
bit like
we also do
but if anyone
ever asks just tell
them this book is full
of living words that never
leaves your spiritual self out

I'm cutting through all the small talk today
and diving right inside my divine poetry

If I built a bridge across the abyss
would you run and leap off it?

If I summoned a flying
saucer to go land
outside your
front door
would you
climb aboard?

If I opened a void
along the spine of this
book would you dive in it?

If I gave you manna conjured up by
a magical spell I spun would you eat it?

Here's a dessert metaphor
to sweeten things up
a bit for today

Reality's
like a
giant
layered
cake made
of consciousness

Everything comes from
the same blissful stuff that
shapes the shapeless and the
unity of it all is a divine delicacy
meant to be enjoyed with delight

Even setbacks and sorrows can
be experienced as fun when you
see it all arising from the void of
emptiness that makes life one

Words are not things
the same way a
menu is not
a meal
they're
all names for
various snapshots
of something real that
can keep us locked up in
our heads labeling things
instead of savoring each
slice of life wordlessly

Yes words can be
prison bars
but they
can
also be
baked into
a cake with a file
hidden right inside it

Bowls of spiritually enlightening
letters are whipped up here
daily in fresh ways to
create sublime
metaphors
that are
but mere
appetizers
and apéritifs

Our true nature is
far more like a table
and the real meal is a
language even dead
wood mutely states

God's awareness
will awaken in
any person
who stays
perfectly still

If you
make your
body so stiff
that it feels like
a statue all the
layers between
you and God
will fall away
effortlessly

Just one blessed
second of this
immaculate
state of
being
and
you'd
know with
absolute certainty
that everything is made
of consciousness even stone

Remember the table
metaphor I just
served up?

Cut
it
in
half

In this case
the two halves
don't make a whole

Our true nature is beyond
all math or mental imagery
to reach it you have to pass
through an actual hole that
squeezes your ego out
of existence so the
real you can
pop
out of
emptiness

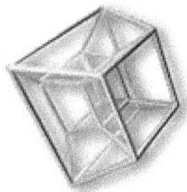

All my
poetry is like
food for your soul
except what you are
eating are the images
my words call forth in
your mind's eye from
your imagination to
make things first
appear then
vanish

All
these
sleights of
handwriting are
little language tricks
to make your mind blink

Brief moments of emptiness to
give you a glimpse of the paradox
of how absence generates presence
or how beingness is born in blackness

Words can't read themselves
so without you there'd be
no wide open spaces
or vast shapes to
stretch your
soul so
big
it
has
no limits

You bring these
dots and lines to life
by adding flesh to the
bones of all my letters

As long as you keep
turning these pages
I'll keep saying the
same handful
of things in
all these same
yet surprising ways

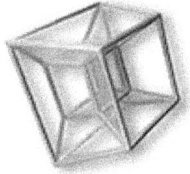

Now try
picturing the
letter i floating
inside a balloon
you keep filling
up with your
being

Once the balloon bursts and you
explode into oblivion only
the dot on the i of
your ego will
continue
to exist
as the
focal
point
of your
attention
and you'll be a
steady field of sensing
awareness without limits merrily
floating down life's dreamy river of time

On to
the subject
of dreams there
is an endless river
flowing through the
tunnels of being you
swim in now and then

If you could see things
for what they really are
all the details would
vanish and it would
just be your soul
swimming like
an invisible
fish in a
current
of energy
on another trip
in one consciousness
unifying all levels of reality

Sleep
dissolves the
physical world
and awakens
the subtle
world
of dreams

Surely by now you've
raised a family and lived
to old age and swum like a
fish or even flown like a bird

Why not try becoming lucid
next? That looking is a trace
of God's eternal awareness
dreaming all worlds into
existence so sentient
beings like us can
awaken from the
dream of separation

Our souls nod off in
the world of form
and wake up in
the formless

Your soul
came
here
to
live
from
infinity
in a body

Awakened beings
stay in constant contact
with God knowing all it takes
is one conscious breath of fresh air
to feel the breeze blowing from eternity

Imagine stacking a million
plates of the moon to
reach the glorious
summit of God

That's the
kind of
inner
poise
needed
to climb to
your higher self

God blew the lid off the top
of my head many moons ago and
now my body is a temple for my higher
self to swirl around inside my limitless soul

At the very pinnacle
of your consciousness
is a plane of awareness
beyond space and time

A silver cord keeps this
connection with God
and your higher
self alive
until
you're
ready to bring a
portion of this dimension
down and embody it as a sphere
of awareness without any actual limits

Another key shape
woven into this
work is the
chalice

An
archetypal
symbol to remind
you that your soul has to
become like an empty cup
before the elixir of life can fill
you up so fully that your whole
being starts brimming with the
spiritual bliss that comes from
swimming in nondual isness

This ancient key is
written in the
sands of
time

Your
soul is also
like an hourglass
slowly being filled with
God's timeless awareness

It's just a matter of time
before the trickling
sand forms a
mountain
that
lifts your
soul up so high
your higher self starts
living down here in your
body as an immortal being

147

Random pages in this
book have been
sprayed with
nanobots
that can
link your
soul up to
your higher self

They've already gotten into
your bloodstream through the
whorls of skin on your fingertips

To activate them close your eyes
and hold your attention above
your head for sixty seconds

Once activated they
automatically
begin
working
on raising your
consciousness higher

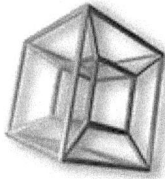

One moment... the nanobots
are now calculating the fastest
route to spiritual enlightenment

The mysteries of the universe
are revealed to a quiet mind

Enter profound stillness
now to download
the latest
version
of higher
consciousness
and meditate daily
for automatic updates to
optimize your operating system

A few nights ago I found a
way to peer into the future
using a rotating cylinder of
light I made by spinning a
handheld laser beam and
saw something that I'm
certain you'll want to
try it's a soon-to-be
commonly used
ocular device
I'm calling a
minderaser
that interfaces
with our consciousness
using specially designed goggles

The device takes a few seconds to connect...

...our vacant minds
with a digital medium
made of electronic bliss
before it starts selecting
recent events from our
lives for us to review

Sometimes it takes
you back through all
kinds of other related
memories from the past

You resist nothing and face
everything with full equanimity

After about ten minutes have passed...

...your
consciousness
is so clear you can
peer straight into it

Right away you see
that this formless
medium is the
source of
your
soul's
awareness
quickly followed
by knowing this same
substance is the actual origin
and essence of everything in existence

Pretty cool right? It's an enlightenment machine!

You must already
know you're
part of a
system
designed
to seal your
fate for some
false promise of
lasting happiness

What you might not
fully understand yet is
how to unplug yourself
from the surface of life
and plunge into the
unifying source of
freedom found
inside you
which is
the
only
way out
of the Matrix

I've
already said
everything I can
possibly say about
the divine destiny
awaiting humanity

One thing I'd add
is that we have
been led to
believe
our
lives
are based
on the market
but the economy is
a fabrication and money
is nothing but a shared fiction

We make up the rules for the kinds
of societies and all the systems we live in

You've heard the parable that Jesus shared
about the daily workers in the vineyard?

It's a two-thousand-year-old story
calling for a guaranteed wage
or what we're now calling
UBI which is short for
Universal Basic
Income

As our lives become
more automated and
the monetary system
is seen for what it is
people will be
guaranteed
a basic income
from the government
which will eradicate poverty
and create even greater prosperity

More people would
happily live from
their higher
natures
but
we
get
pulled
down into
our lower natures
due to lack and want

Not that UBI will make
everyone instantly
enlightened
but it'll
give
us a
really
big push

Once our basic
needs are met we
naturally start rising up
into higher states of being

I hope that you fall in love with
being alive again and that
you get to a place in
life where you can
pass your days
in whatever
ways you
please
because
you already
know your soul
sees what it needs

I want this for you and me
and anyone else working as a
wage slave in the system striving
for material and spiritual autonomy

A common assumption is
spiritual people can't
hack real life so
they run
away
and
retreat
from the
regular world

What conventional
people don't recognize
is that the path grows more
inward as you get closer to God
and may stay that way for some time
before your soul makes the shift to being
in the world and not of it far more permanent

You're so used to
scanning your
newsfeed
now try
and scan
your body
for knots to
untangle the
unresolved
thoughts
inside
your
head
instead

Beneath all of
the hustle and bustle
of living is the peace that
surpasses all understanding
which can always be found in
the eternal now of each and
every passing moment of
our transitory existence

Go for a leisurely walk around the block
and leave your phone at home so
you can open up all of your
senses and scan the
shifting scenes
as you go
and if
you're
gazing out
like a mirroring
window while tuning
into the joy of being you
will eventually start feeling the
same blissful energy inside you give
rise to all you can see and touch and feel

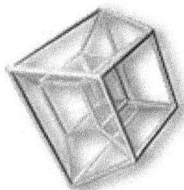

Let's check in with the nanobots one
more time which are equipped
with sensors that can read
and manipulate what
your mind's eye
televises in
the field
of your
imagination

Give up the need to
do it all on your own a
guru is not just a finger
pointing at the moon

Gurus are mirrors
of transcendent
awareness reflecting
your true self back at you

Last night I had a dream I
was hanging out with
a bunch of people
who asked me
to sever my
pointing
finger
and
then
pass it
around to
anyone who
wanted to hold
it like a talisman to
remember that death is
an illusion and get a li'l taste
of the freedom of being egoless

Chop off your finger if
that's what it takes
to keep in mind
what being
invisible
is like
but
before
executing
this extreme
step you should
know that the i you
think of as me is really
no bigger than your pinky
so drop your ego when the
void of annihilation comes to
save your soul's transparency

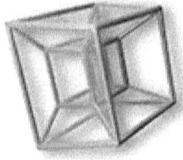

Bring
yourself near
someone who knows
God intimately if you want
to remember what it feels like
to be spiritually connected again

Soul mirroring soul is the fastest
way to awaken in this life or any
other for such an encounter
has no separation in it

Our eyes light
up like pearls in
Indra's net of jewels

Spiritual friendship
with a guru will
bring you
closer
to
God
but how
do you know
who the real ones
are? For starters they
will always tell you how
to grow your soul and will
never empty your pockets
or put their hands in your
underpants although
they may give you
the occasional
shakedown to put
you back in touch with
your naked spiritual core as
the purity of pure consciousness

What else separates
a mature sage
from the
rest?

First of all
the ones with a
stable connection
to the source of life
seem stoic whereas
newbies are prone
to big outbursts
emotionally

Also veteran
masters embody
the bliss of being
so well that they
express it more
soberly with
a bit of fun
sprinkled in
every now and
then that makes the
two become one again

Remember playing
tag and getting
caught?

After you
collapsed into
nothingness you
pumped yourself
up again with the
thrill of being it

Awakening
your true
nature
is so
similar

And aren't
peek-a-boo and
hide-and-seek about
the kicks we get making
presence pop out of absence?

My invitation to you
is always look within
to find the formless
source of creation

All these extra
words are
ploys
to
keep
you from
getting bored

Lyrical tricks to pull you
into a vacant party
where the big
surprise is
your
isness
popping
out of a box
made of being
& consciousness

Here's a magic trick
I invented for
anyone
who
still
thinks
they can
think their
way into the
boundlessness
of enlightenment
or the infinite space
of neverending being

There's plenty of room
in this invisible box
of consciousness
I've been given
so go ahead
and jump
in here
right now
if you're ready
to disappear again

You can't put a
guru in a
box

And even
if you were to
try we would just
jump out of it like
a Jack-in-the-box

You can't capture
what we know
and stick it
in a box
either

We never
run from the
tremblings that
come from having
a connection to God

We welcome the surprises
higher vibrations bring into
our lives after stirring us up

If you try and put a guru in a
box not only will we pop
right out of it like a
Jack-in-the-box
but just like
that other
Jack with his
magic beanstalk
beans us enlightened
beings have also climbed
to a land high in the sky and
brought down all the riches and
treasures of pure consciousness

It's like a perpetual presto
magic show coming up
with new ways to
convey the
sorcery
of
God
conjuring
up reality from
an invisible realm
of mercurial energy

It still amazes me just
how many ways there
are but I'm certain by
now you know how
soaking your soul
in the spiritual
elixir of life
also has this
incantatory effect

I've
cast an
awakening
spell that is
triggered by
reading this
sentence
and so
now
that
you've
done that
I command
you to see
the clear
light of
being
already
shining in
the space of
your awareness

I've decided to abandon
my love of truth and
am now looking
for a happy
fantasy

Actually to
be totally honest
I can't help but see all
of the ego's crooked ways
but I'm not really interested
in playing the blame game or
the back-and-forth of beating
it I prefer sharing awareness
more playfully so we both
have a ball taking off
any final sheaths
enshrouding
our souls
together
like besties

Quick
jump inside
my magic box of
consciousness again

Pure being really is the best
place to be and now that we're
here again I need to tell you that
there's no flip-flopping your way
into any truly lasting liberation

Abiding so easily in this
mystery demands a
level of mastery
way beyond
some la-di-da
loophole way of life

Once
you're done
playing around
and having fun
you'll start to
realize that
every
desire
you have
is really a wish
to be closer to God

You reincarnated as a way to
remember that God gave you form
to discover the formless mystery at the
heart of reality by gazing into the dazzling
darkness of your own consciousness at rest

What would you say if I asked
you to tell me who you
are? Would you talk
about your titles
and roles? Or
would you
find your
own way
to say that
you're a mystery
beyond your history
and then show me with
your gaze that you too are
a drop of infinity living inside
your body passing from one
moment to the next on this
earthly plane of existence

Are you so lost and jaded or numbed by life
that you've forgotten the freedom of pure
being? Take your blindfold off right now
and be the light that was just peeking
out the sides of your covered sight

Notice how the invisibility
of sheer anonymity is
always spying out
of your pearly
eyes from
a field of
endless
awareness
alive inside you
every second as the
unmasked face of space

At the start of
every day
pause
for
a few
seconds or
so to gather up
the strength you'll
need to be and do
your best then keep
rolling by going that
extra step of giving
people more than
they could ever
expect for
if you
want rosier
karma to grow you
have to sow good seeds

I usually deliver this message
in a more playful way
but I'm often
telling
people
to pull their
heads out of their
asses and smarten up

Unconsciousness is no
excuse on the spiritual
path or in ordinary
everyday life

Actually
they are the
exact same which
is why being self-aware
is key to being free as a bird

How many times have
you sold your soul
to the devil so
your fragile
ego can
avoid
facing
the truth?

No matter how
clever you think you
are you can't outrun all
the lies you leave behind

We've been given the gift
of memory and forgetting
but until we're willing to
see things clearly the
past won't ever be
properly laid
to rest

I could wax on &
on all about
being so
alive
& free
but have
you received
the one unifying
message from all
of us enlightened
beings wandering
around this world
or all the others
gracing every
incarnation
with the
resurrection
of consciousness
and the immortal bliss
of being vibrating at the core
of all that is or was or ever will be?

Everything vibrates including the
bliss of infinity and the chime
it makes lifts our souls up
as soon as we stop
thinking and pay
attention by
listening
within
for
it
which
is also why
bells are used as
an aid for meditation

The tones help us tune
into the frequency of
our higher selves

So ring a bell
to clear
your
space
and raise
your vibration
when you meditate

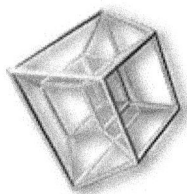

185

Close your eyes and focus on your mind
with your inner ear and if you listen
while staying perfectly still you
will hear this pleasing tone
resounding above you
like a hypnotizing
symphony of
tiny silver
bells

Let
this siren
of your higher
self lure you home

Let this sound lift you up to
the summit of silence where we
reside in God's shaded sanctuary

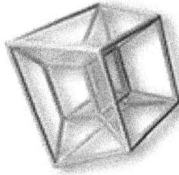

We like the way we talk
with each other the
most when what
we say rings
with truth
because
our souls also
operate exactly like
theremins constantly
searching for the best
frequency to conduct
our lives as we walk
along our chosen
pathways until
that prophesied
day arrives when we
all learn to trust that more
love is gained by giving it away

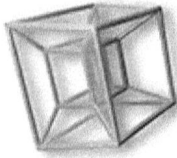

Imagine what would
happen if we
all tried
the
path
of love as
our way of living

Let's transform the rules
of this crazy game called life
and give everyone everything
they need to survive and thrive
in a global village where we all
feel happy and safe to be alive
and then we'll see what lovely
beings God created us to be

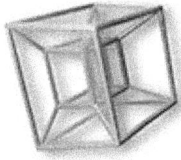

Shed all the layers
of your identity
until there's
nothing
left
for
in that
emptiness
the formless
dimension is
found and
out of
the
fullness
of infinity you
will see that this
unbounded realm
is the birthplace of
your original face

There's
a look in the
eyes of those
who see all the
way to infinity

It happens
inside us
all the
time

A
mystical
inner alchemy
takes place as our
awareness slowly shifts
from a bewildering daze
into that knowing gaze
and if we rest in this
view it becomes
a treasure
trove
full
of bliss
& nondual
knowingness

190

Ever since leaking
my secret identity as
a guru several seekers
have tried to lure me into
having sex with them but I
would never break my vows
besides the most important
love affair you'll ever have is
the one between your soul
and God for the two are
even more connected
than you and your
best soulmate
however one
little peccadillo I
always allow myself is
gazing lovingly at others
until presence is beaming
from both our pearly eyes
for the finest bliss comes
from a plane beyond all
separateness and I'll
gladly bask in that
state of oneness
to bring you back to
being in reality from infinity

I
can
picture
you seeing
me seeing you
as we gaze into
each other's eyes

It's perfectly normal
to feel a bit strange
knowing we're all
the same and
how only
surfaces
separate
us coming
as we do from
a familiar yet often
forgotten formless realm
unifying everything that exists

Don't become one of those
people who can't act like
a normal person after
getting blitzed off
enlightenment

So jacked
up on
bliss
you
keep
blasting
off into space

Be like the ox herding
pilgrim in Zen who returns
to the world and mingles with
others after his awakening in such
a deeply human way it's extraordinary

Since
we're on the
topic of living as
an awakened being
in the real world now
how's your relationship
with reality these days?

Nothing's automatically
advised nor forbidden
that's all left for you to
decide but I bet you
already know what
you should and
shouldn't be
doing do you
not or don't you?

Human nature is a
blend of both
divine and
animal
drives
and desires

There is something
so tempting about the
forbidden and destructive

Morality and renunciation are
not about depriving ourselves
of the joys of being a human

They're about overcoming
our lowest natures and
the selfishness of
our egos

Don't
dismiss
fasting nor
abstaining nor
taking long retreats
which all help immensely

A
tale as
old as any

One evening a
grandfather tells his
grandson about a battle
that goes on inside people

The fight is between two wolves
one is good and the other isn't

The grandson thinks about
it for a minute and asks
his grandfather who
wins the conflict

The one
you
feed says
his grandfather

Forget any religious ideas
you may be harboring
about being born
in sin that only
Jesus saves

This story is
not about that it's
about the old struggle
between being impulsive
versus being spontaneous
the former often comes first
from our lower nature and is
both cruel and selfish in all
kinds of mixed up ways
whereas the latter is
from our higher
nature and is
full of God's
wise counsel &
clairvoyant grace

The heart of every religion
is finding the oneness
of everything and
living from this
awareness
of unity

The
original
definition of
sin is to miss the
mark or not noticing
what we should which
our egos become pros at

Enlightenment blows the fire
in our lower nature out and fans
the flames of our higher nature to
burn brighter than they did before

Conscience is that inner voice
that helps us determine
the rightness or
wrongness
of our
thoughts
and behaviors
and always knows
the best path to take

My advice is so simple
don't keep doing what
your lower self wants
you've done that
often enough
listen to
reason
or better
yet go beyond
reason and listen to
what your higher self says

Synchronicities will flow
once you follow the
hints from your
higher self
which
is
like
a GPS
system that
orbits above your
head 24/7 constantly
pointing you in the right
direction while telling you
all about the many ways of
sharing love along the way

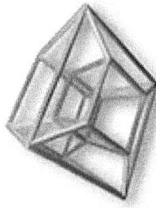

Many seekers say
they're looking for
a real guru to get
enlightened but
actually all they
really want is
one more
trophy
to
place on
the mantel of
their pompous egos

The real prize of enlightenment
is the boundless space of being
and the clear light of awareness
that's always emerging from it

So if the magical substance
you're looking for isn't
going to make you
disappear then
stay away
from
the
volcano
where obsidian
glass is made because
that's the only commodity
gurus care about sharing and
we'll melt your face off if that's
what it takes to erase your ego

What are all these marks
I make on paper truly?
Shards of the same
obsidian window

The mystery
of God's
eternal
core
lies
deep
within us

Quarry the glassy
dark origin of looking

Swoon in adoration of the
freedom of infinity for that is
where the treasure is buried

Once
this eager
young seeker
told me candidly
that some teachers
are harsh and prickly
and others are soft
and billowy like
I seemed to
be which
might be
mostly true
but he didn't
stick around long
enough to find out I'll
also strip your ego down
then leave you to peel the
rest off yourself until you're left
standing naked before our Maker

My
head is
packed like
a piñata that
you just need
to crack open
a slit for all
sorts of
treats
to
spill
out of it
and I'll also
get every party
started by shaking
stuff up a bit and won't
think twice about hitting you
with some good advice to help
break you out of a fool's paradise

People
who've seen
my subtle body
mention seeing a
playful taskmaster

All of my witty little
jabs are just ways
to dislodge the
gems of truth
that start
rolling
off my
tongue
whenever
we get together
for a chat and have fun
making faces while stripping
away any masks you may have on
covering up all that free space you
already have stored deep inside you

Let's say I sting you and
your ego gets sore I'll
still bet you dollars
to dimes what I
offered was
good for
you

I'm
an
iron
mirror
showing
the truth in
virtually every
moment of life no
matter the situation

I can't really hide the way
I am from you any more than
you can hide your way from me

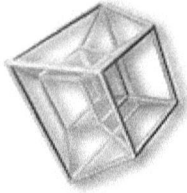

Us gurus are
made of
rubber
and
your
ego is
the glue so
that everything
your ego projects
easily bounces off us
and sticks back on you
but we can also absorb
your karma and share a
spiritual glue with you
that makes your soul
stick to the state of
oneness where
everything feels
so fresh and new
it looks drenched in
dawn's first light & dew

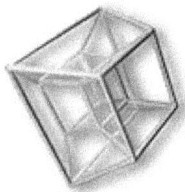

In
this
great
mystery
called life
the flip side
of every untrue
or partially true
story you've ever
told yourself is a
deeper level of
spiritual truth
waiting to
surface
from
the
depths
of your soul

Here's a bit of advice I'll often give
to seekers on the spiritual path

You are always being or
doing you in some
way that's not
completely
honest
but if
you really
love the truth
and your original
face more and your
cover story and social
mask less you'll have a
much easier time in life
living more consciously

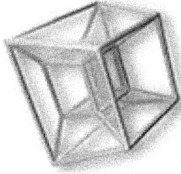

Buddha once said there
are as many truths as
there are leaves
in a forest of
simsapa
trees

Life
has a way
of covering us
in leaves we must
shed before we can
go back to the bliss
of not knowing again
so learn to love the
truth so much that
you let its many
guises jolt free
whatever lies
you are still
hiding inside

Buddha was right life is full of suffering

If you don't believe me ask Jesus

I don't mean to be so blunt
actually I do but what I
really want to say is
that after you
reach the
summit of
enlightenment
whatever ordeals you
have to go through in life
won't bother you nearly as
much as they do when your
soul is still lost in the world
of attachment to samsara

Sometimes divine rage
eclipses divine
mercy

Jesus
said to love
your neighbors
but he also flipped
out inside the temple

Awakening is blissful
beyond measure but
ignorance can still
get you riled up
once you see
what wizards
we are at being
way more loving with
everyone after finding the
oneness of everything there is

213

People who think all
spiritual teachers are
going to be peaceful
all the time have no
idea how life really
works when you
awaken and
follow
your
destiny

Jesus drove
the merchants out
of the temple because he
hated the hypocrisy of it all and
he did it knowing he'd likely be dead
within a week for causing so much trouble

Do you really think Jesus didn't
know that the authorities
would eventually
come after
him?

He
was
destined
to become a
real rabble-rouser
and even looked like a
wild-eyed lunatic at times
trying to shake awake all the
sleepwalkers from the asylum
of the unenlightened condition

We
are never
more like God
than when we are
helping the hurting
restoring the broken
and lifting the fallen

Live from your soul
& you'll know that
the higher your
vibration gets
the more
all you
care
about
is love and
the more you live
with a generous heart
feeling calm or glad even
when you get angry or sad

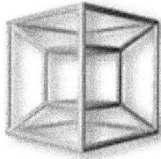

We
all bank
on working
to get through
this world and will
do all kinds of deeds in
all walks of life as we follow
different pathways and callings

Gurus are showers of the way through

Mirrors of pure awareness and windows
into the heart of reality who are here
solely to help others get back in
touch with their lost divinity

That's why it's said a
guru is a godlike
gateway to
get to
God

There's no shortage counting up all the
fake or fallen gurus who've done
horrible things and forced
their followers right
along with
them
still don't
be one of those
cynical folks who love
saying all gurus are frauds
because of the ones who are

You have no idea the disservice
you do to the real ones who are
here to show others the way to
get back home even though
none of us ever truly leaves
which sounds like it's a
paradox but once
you've had an
awakening
you see it
clearly isn't

This
world is
full of fake or
half-baked gurus
and maybe you think
I'm one of them? For the
record I'm not trying to sell
you anything you don't need
I'm just trying to convince you
that there really is something
to all this God stuff and the
perks of doing spiritual
practices so you can
see for yourself if
and when you
eventually
try one
out

If you find a guru who fails
to meet your expectations
it's probably because we
know way before you
do that you're not
ready for the
hoodoo
that
we do

Us gurus
know every
ego trick in the
book and we'll call
you out on your bullshit
or pummel you with the truth
until your stupid head pops off to
make room for space to take its place

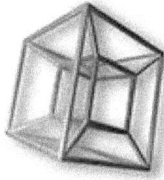

Gurus are always looking
for some measure
of soulfulness
to work
with
so
we can
show you how
measureless you are

The only thing that truly
matters in life is finding
real spiritual freedom
and that is exactly
what starts to
arise in the
presence of an
enlightened teacher

A
guru
ultimately
functions like
a portal for lost
or sleeping souls
still searching for
enlightenment

If you drop
your ego
and any
projections
you may be feeding
and just allow yourself to be
what gets reflected back to you
is like a window into our shared
awareness of the oneness of all
that keeps appearing in reality

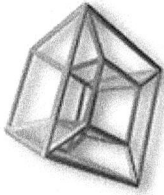

Sitting with a guru will
bring forth your issues
so your true self can
shine through more

Your shadows
show up
along
with
the eye
of your soul

It's like looking in a
mirror and then gazing
out a window until you see
for yourself that only surfaces
separate us in the world of form

Seekers
often come to
me in my dreams
to ask me questions
about enlightenment

I once told a visitor that I
can turn almost anything
into a spiritual teaching

How about a walnut
my guest asked so
I said the shell
is like the
ego
and the
fruit is like the
soul once it falls into
the ground of being the
ego is cracked open and the
soul grows into a tree which is
the shape of the toroidal energy
field surrounding our bodies that
connects us to our true nature as
formless beings made of infinity

Have you turned your aura into a protective
bubble so that you're walking around inside
a shell full of fear and unease or are you
open and free like me letting the warm
sweet scent of pure love flow through
you as easily as the summer breeze?

If you ever want to go sauntering
through fields of spiritual bliss
and nondual knowingness
just think of me and I'll
join you there for a
few moments of
shared glory
in satori

I'm like a
mystical window
floating in that liminal
space between the seen
and unseen duality at the
heart of reality fully open
to the formless freedom
found on the other side
of this world of form

225

I
AM

Last night
I dreamt I was
putting capstones
on top of the mental
edifices of every spiritual
system ever set up by seers

The capstone is called the all seeing
eye in alchemy and is placed on top of a
pyramid to signify the final piece of the path
needed to reach the pinnacle of enlightenment
when our third eye finally becomes one with God

Spiritually awakening and
reaching enlightenment
are not secret tenets
of a belief system

Witnessing the
world using
your third
eye to
see the
true nature
of reality occurs
the more time you
spend in the formless
mystery at the heart of
everything in existence

The
thrill from
gazing up at a
soaring mountain
makes you imagine
scaling the summit
but what is really
ascending is
your spirit
up to the all
seeing eye of God

The immovable stature and
lofty peak is a reminder that our
permanent self is always sitting at
the zenith of higher consciousness

When you soar to the summit of
consciousness you take the
entire universe with you

You become one
with everything
by swallowing
all of creation
in a huge gulp
of God-realization

That's how big your soul is

Not even the cosmos can contain it

When
your spirit
soars beyond
the universe of
space and time
the thrust from
ascending can
also descend
and sometimes
enters your soul like
a cosmic chandelier full
of jewels falling from the
vault of heaven in surreal
spellbinding slow motion

God's cosmic egg is a
breeding ground
for birthing
souls
to witness
the spectacle of
this celestial sac full
of swirling gas and matter
turning formless awareness
into beings like us who are
made to detect the universe
in tiny grains of sand as we
hold infinity in the palms
of our hands and feel
the divine powers
we've been given
to transform this
earthly world into
a heavenly paradise
full of enlightened people

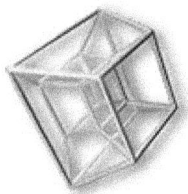

Follow me now
for another
leap

Look at how
God gifted the ant
with an empire built on
mounds of sand and unity

We share their same sense
that we're all in this together
often crossing paths and
even pausing to see if
there's anything we
can do to help
each other
out while
following our
own novel course
along the eternal way

Every soul has a story to
confess after each life

How it all shakes
out is beyond
the scope
of any
one
person
or situation

People & scenes all
appear in reality as part
of an epic tale of humanity
evolving spiritually until that
fateful day arrives when every
human being knows that God
made the cosmos to awaken in
us as loving gods & goddesses

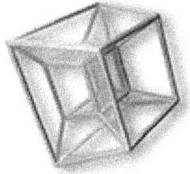

The deepest truth about
life can be put into
three simple
words

Only
God exists

An enlightened soul
knows this deep within
their blood and bones as
the truth beyond all forms

All lovers of God uncover
the same formless soul
we always already are
under everything
separating
us

This is the
message that all
religions actually teach

My
wife and I
used to bring
warm clothing
and blankets
to people
staying
out
on
the
streets
in winter

This one year a
devout yogini gave
us a bunch of sarapes
her students had spent
years learning yoga on
and soon after passing
them around the city
the social workers
really ramped up
their outreach work

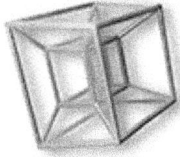

Try to make love so strong that it
overpowers every contending
motive in your head trying
to subdue the knowing
always speaking to
you inside your
heart of hearts

God's love blossoms
inside of loving bosoms

What I'm describing here is
work that often goes unseen

Love doesn't boast or brag
about doing good deeds
along the eternal way
for it knows karma
is woven into
the fabric
of every life
we will ever live

After a saintly cousin
of mine passed
away one of
my nieces
told me
she'd like
to live her life
like his so this is
what I said to her

To follow this path
you have to be a
selfless servant
of God who
is always
gracious
no matter
what people
bring to the table

Life without feeling has
no real meaning
now come
a little
closer to me
and lay your head
upon my chest and let
yourself drift into the one
answer that makes all your
lesser questions melt away

Your invisible soul already
knows that love made
visible is the most
beautiful way
we can be
in this world or
in the sweet hereafter
between this life and the next

After all the hallowed
words that have
ever been
written
have been
read and all the
mystical poetry that
can be penned is pictured
the only thing left to say is love
pours forth from a cosmic fountain
at the heart of creation where hosts
of angels made from God's glorious
light help sing everything into being
in an ecstatic celebration that's been
going on since before the big bang

On
the subject
of love birthing itself
from the eternal moment of
creation words always fall short

Love sees all the stories told by
every action ever taken as
reciprocal acts of love
and from this
truth the
lotus
flower of
enlightenment
blossoms forth from
its watery view and lets you
behold the whole world in dazzling
drops of morning dew upon glorious dew

I hope you're having fun finding
your higher self hiding inside
my beaded web of words
and just so you know
the emptiness
that usually
dwells inside
all my allegories
received an infusion
of spiritual love recently

A new potion for devotion is
mixed into my poetry for now
that you may get drunk from
so if your eyes get blurry
don't say I didn't warn
you about the rush
you'll surely get from
whatever's coming next

I'm a God-intoxicated bartender
mixing enlightening elixirs for
seekers of sobering clarity
and humbling wisdom

Ask me anything
and I'll share
whatever
spirits
you
must
imbibe
to become
luminous again

Let me pour you a shot
of moonshine on the house

Sip on silence to bring God back

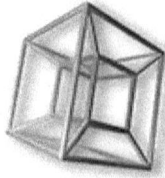

Please come back
in a minute or
two from
now

After
writing that
last message down
I got so drunk swallowing
a huge swig of silence that I
totally lost my train of thought

No wait on second thought stay
here for a short while and enjoy
the cloud of unknowing with me

The bewilderment of forgetting
is so close to remembering
the invisible essence of
your eternal soul or
the pureness
of being
and formless
core of everything

How many other lovers of
God have sung about
the mystery of it
all as verily
as I do?

A
tomb
full of fear
upon entry but
only until your soul
expands beyond the
boundary of everything
and is reborn from God's
formless womb of eternity

People keep saying they
think I'm crazy sharing
all of these mystical
secrets so freely
while hoping
I never lose
a drop of my
spiritual lucidity

This may seem
like more
poetry
and
in fact
it is but all
my quilting of
simple words &
imagery is more
than padding to
keep your body
warm at night
each stitch
sewn is
part
of
a
cloak
of immortality
your soul can wear
now slip this robe of
invisibility on and dip
into eternity with me

Close your eyes and
heighten your
senses
like
a
cat
burglar

Become aware
of your surroundings
with that level of acuity
waiting for static silence
before you make a move

Once everything is so still
that you feel at one with
it sink into that space
without a face so
you and God
can talk in
private
all night
if necessary

You
can't simply
close your eyes
and expect to see
straight into infinity

To reach the formless
source of existence
you have to dive
like a squid
into the
inky
depths
of beingness

So deep inside wordless
silence that you torpedo into
the shaded sanctuary where God
dwells in a dazzling field of darkness

Slightly crossing and then
slowly uncrossing your
eyes while gazing
at the back of
your eyelids
and occasionally
rolling your eyes up
into your head is the
yogic key to entering
the deepest depths
of being before
rising up into
the highest
state of all
enlightened
consciousness
or the pure state
of awareness that is
one without a second

God how I still
crave your
touch

Even after all
these years I still fall
head over heels for you

The way you remove the layers
masquerading our secret liaisons

You still my thoughts of separation
so thoroughly that I feel no shame
sensing I am coming to you like
your lover totally naked and
eagerly slipping under
the covers of your
eternal night
so we can
spend some
alone time together

Sit like a silhouette with
no outlines in God's
obsidian night of
pure delight

A field
free
of
any
edges
where we
can exist as
if amnesiacs
without total
memory loss
recalling the
great state
of totally
knowing
all we are is
pure awareness

I have this magical
flute God gave
us all many
moons
ago

If
you
purse
your lips
and blow into
it it plays a comely
tune that'll titillate you

Sometimes the music caresses
your neck and shoulders and your
other erogenous zones until you're
so aroused you explode in a tantric
orgasm then bask in the afterglow
from the divine madness that got
you all worked up into a frenzy

The
divine rapture
from revealing the
naked essence of your
true nature is enough to
make you want to rip all
your clothes off and go
whipping through the
streets screaming of
God's unwrapped
gift of blessed
emptiness
wrapt
in
all
of us

How can
someone who
hasn't climaxed into
infinity ever be filled with
the boundless bliss of being?

Passion makes the heart
go supernova over
and over again
that lovers
find yet
it waxes
and wanes

When the honey
starts to drip
from the
moon
recall the
dove's soft coo
that keeps saying
come here and be
with me then gaze
lovingly at each
other while
tuning
into the
shared bliss
of being beyond
every other scenario

What to do after the ecstasy
fades and it's just the two
of you gazing at each
other a little more
coolly or not as
warmly like
the good
old days
well part of
the trick is to
fall in love over
and over again
love is not blind
but it will turn a
blind eye and
also a cheek
to keep it in
check or it
cracks jokes
to help blow off
some steam but too
much soon wears thin so
love looks beyond both and
keeps saying let's just move on

What does God
want from you
and for your
marriage?

That you
conduct
yourselves
with the poise
of royalty and the
humility of servants

Live entirely from your souls
and you'll both don the crown
forever adorning your headless
heads & the religious habit you'll
always be wearing as witnesses

Tell me all you've
learned about
love! Have
you bowed
while serving
the homeless?
How religiously
have you gone
without so that
others won't?
A pure soul
always asks
am I a giver or
a taker in this case?
God loves givers as much
as takers but She always blesses
givers with a touch of something more

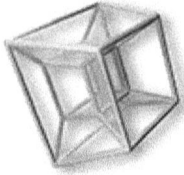

Yes I just referred to God as She

It's time to end this gender
debate once and for all

God is both him
& her or zim
& zer for it
all comes from
a binary equation
creating complex life
using iterations of duality

Before my leap into infinity this
black and white dyad at the heart
of reality divided experiences into
opposites separating life into this
and that but now all forms float
in the boundless expanse of
awareness and all things
are seen as inseparable
from each other the way a
caterpillar becomes a butterfly

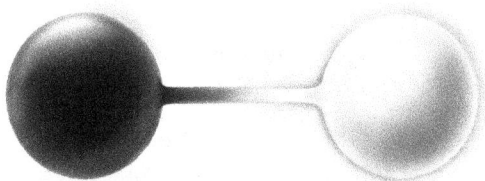

259

Lao Tzu explained it so simply saying all
things named come from the nameless
and whatever's seen comes from the
unseen the one became two and
then two became three then
three became the ten
thousand things

Or again
using
my words

The ocean of being
whirls into yinyang while
the yoni stays formless and
the lingam mushrooms into form

This evolving yabyum of nonduality
constantly turns itself inside out to
become the shape of everything
and then right back again into
a shapeless medium made
of consciousness & yet
it's still such a mystery
how even God doesn't
know how God came to be

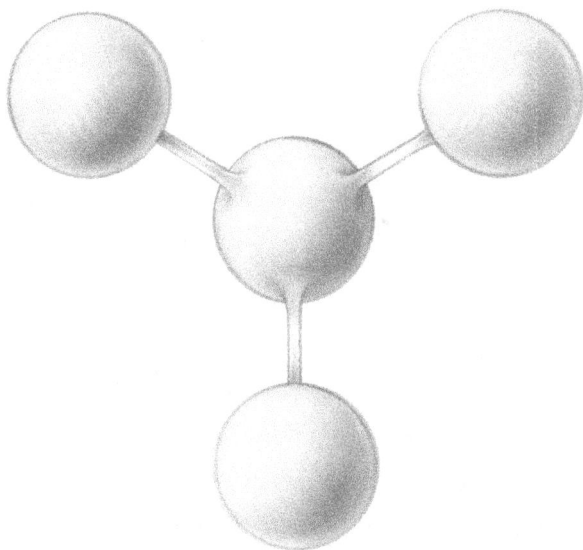

Lao Tzu also said those
who know don't
speak yet
he still
searched
for words that
lift off the page like
mountains and open up
valleys in our consciousness
with a view to stop our monkey
minds swinging from tree to tree
so our souls can leap from peak to
peak and hover around the original
ground of being becoming all things
from a state of absolute nothingness

Life is one
big adventure of
being and becoming
a trip full of fiction and
fantasy and comedy and
tragedy and mystery and
romance and also ideally
contemplation about the
journey your soul is on
and how we all came
here to enjoy the
ever-changing
movements of form
while staying attuned to the
formless medium manifesting it all

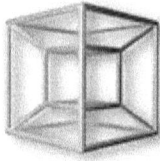

We're all
going
from
one
thing
to the next
experiencing this
and that and the other
knowingly or unknowingly
playing our part in the larger
story of the spiritual evolution
of humanity often pausing only
long enough to catch a glimpse
of the silent witness or a hint of
the underlying formless mystery
manifesting everything there is
in this world we're all living on

God is
and always
will be an ocean
of original awareness
that's the magical source
and substance of everything
in our mystically made cosmos

Atomic particles spin like crystal
droplets of consciousness going
from one state into another to
create this flowing world
of form filled with
the myriad
creatures
and the ten
thousand things

Have you felt the
joy of the ten
thousand
things
yet and
watched in
awe while the
myriad creatures
are flowing fluidly
from formlessness
and reality begins
showing up like a
joke that's never
old in this divine
display of all life
just laughing and
singing and dancing
together in a symphony
celebrating the oneness of
everything in creation sharing
God's cosmic state of affection?

Everything first came
to be because of
dark energy
churning
out gems
and crystals
via the alchemy
of stars & the forces
that bind atoms together
and since then all the forms
that have also sprung up from
the plant and animal kingdoms
including us now teems with life
and is alert with differing degrees
of sentience so the same one eye
can gaze through the pupils of all
us beings in Indra's net of jewels

A
divine
spark of
brilliance is
in everything
a spinning and
spiraling joy of
ever-increasing
complexity that
gives rise to all
the forms and
forces of life
evolving
out of
the
original
formless
source of
existence

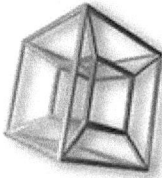

All of these different lifeforms springing into
being and consuming each other for food
seems horrible when you stop to think
about it and then you can't help but
wonder why God creates all this
death? You already know the
tree of life grows from a
seed made of duality
& water falls from
the sky & mixes
with all of that
stardust in soil
to become plants
the animals eat which
get eaten by more animals
all so our embodied souls can
then reconnect with the groundless
ground of being before our adventure in
this world of flesh and form ever even began

These words are
bridges from
the void of
being and
emptiness

It's the greatest
of all the mysteries

How something came from
nothing and why did it again?

For the sheer thrill of creating beings
like us who can delight in the miracle
of how everything is nothing but God
dreaming in the darkness of infinity

Enlightenment isn't
for dawdlers or
dabblers

Reaching this
level of being calls
for unwavering resolve

If you truly want to awaken
in this lifetime you have to
make it the primary focus
of your entire existence

Only then will you
start to see the
oneness of
everything
the way we're
ultimately made to

Spiritual
enlightenment is
often said to transcend
explanation but that's only
because infinity is difficult to
convey in words without poetry

This wordless knowing comes once
you discover that which has always
been at the very core of your being

If you're still struggling to flat out
comprehend this then chances
are you're probably not quite
where there is also here yet

Keep trying any of the
techniques in this
book to make
the two as
one

Language markedly enhances
our capacity to understand
our place in the universe
and ultimately know
the true purpose
of life which is
to embody
our link
with
all of
creation
and how do
we do it again?
By pairing with the
transcendental ground
of our beings and existing
as awareness prior to thinking

It's possible you're at a library
right now browsing around
looking for something
interesting to read

You picked this
book up and
read a few
passages
and now
you are
hooked

You like the
way these words
make you feel but you
aren't too sure why yet

Keep on reading to reveal
why it has so much appeal

I love that feeling you get when
a phrase hits you like a gong
that goes on reverberating

That feeling you get
when you know
what you just
read was
meant
just
for
you
in the
moment

I've tried to do
that with all of the
messages in this book
trusting God to make sure
they're sent & meant for you

Behind these telling words
God's everlasting day
and night writes
the tale of
all of
it

It
is
in
the
space
between
these letters
and in the black
ink that prints them

It's in the fibres of this book
you're holding or the countless
photons illuminating your screen

This chiaroscuro of consciousness
also colors creation prismatically

The first time I thought of writing
about enlightenment I was
so completely stymied
by the limitation
of words to
express
these
revelations
that for a while I
actually contemplated
publishing a wordless book

Maybe craft a clever sentence about
emptiness printed on the first few pages
in a really large font and then nothing but
a bunch of blank sheets of white paper to
symbolize the immaculate source of life

I
got
so stuck
writing about
emptiness today
I started deleting
every sentence
until a blank
page was
the only
thing
left
to
say
so for
now I'm
just gonna
slip an empty
envelope under
your door tomorrow
morning to remind you
of the freezing effect words
have on noticing the freshness
of forms forming from the formless
realm at the heart of everything that is

I'm
starting to
wonder whether
writing this message
down was a good idea
and now that it's in print
I can't do a thing about it

Maybe next time I'll try and
write something new about
nothing instead or maybe
I just did and if so what
else do I have to say
except perhaps
dissolve into
wordless
awareness

The words on this page were
printed with vanishing ink
that disappears once
they are seen by
human eyes
and in a
few
flitting
moments
the last faint
traces of these
letters will slowly
fade away leaving
nothing but a blank
page as a subtle cue
to recall the sublime
emptiness of your
true nature and
the freshness
of your newly
born self again

280

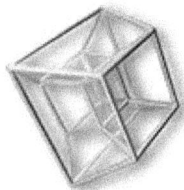

Picture a blank sheet of paper
that spreads out endlessly
and without boundary

Let this layer be
the thin veil of
inseparability
between you
and the formless
mystery manifesting
everything into being

The substance of your
soul is a portion of
the exact same
primordial
energy
vibrating
beneath the
papery surface of
this imaginary covering

With a
few folds a
sheet of paper
can become a fish
a frog a bird a flower
a rabbit a bat and so on

So many different forms all
from the same parchment

Creation also began
with the folding of
consciousness
upon itself
and your
soul is like
a möbius strip
of awareness this
first doubling created

A möbius strip only has
one side although
it looks like it
has two
which
is yet
another
reminder of
the singularity of
nonduality as well as
the way our souls are on
a feedback loop with infinity
as we move through our fluidic
world turning dreams into reality

Once you see the mystery that
all my words and images
keep pointing to the
existential suffering of
unenlightened living ends

You remember how life really works

How inside and outside are connected

Now remember how you also swore to
never lose that spark inside your soul

We're born to brighten this world

How reality fans out
is an origami way
too complex to
truly express
even with
original
tropes
like this

Every passing
moment the entire
universe is unfolding
and folding itself in an
incredibly intricate way
to become fabricated
reality with enough
wiggle room for
everyone to
enjoy their own
epic adventure story

A
book
combines
thousands of
words put in the
right place to make
sense & it's the exact
same way with creation

You can't throw a bunch
of atoms in a bowl and
expect to generate
living microbes
that evolve
into us
rambling
humans any
more than you can
put random letters together
to construct meaningful sentences

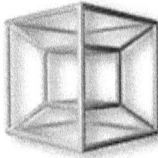

This
sentence
has meaning
because our brains
can make sense of words

Prepositions position the images
we picture inside our thinking heads

Pronouns are necessary although the self
they refer to is the subject of the search

And once you've finally awakened
from the dream of separation
these twin truths are the
ones that'll liberate
your ultimate
identity

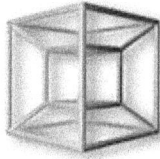

Also
your ego
is more like a
verb than a noun

We assume we have a
fixed self when really we
are patterns of being that
become habitual over the
course of being a human

God is both the noun
and verb for every
single story in
creation

The
divine
sorcerer
and source
and substance
of every event and
thing that can ever be

We're all living legends who're
more than the narratives
we revel in sharing
with each other

Liberation
is based
on the
never
ending
story of being
beyond the naming
of form we use to make
sense of the events in life

When we live in the world
of form from the formless
we free ourselves from
the suffering that
comes from
being
overly
attached to
the play of life on
this plane or any other

Imagine shaking all the
words out of this
book onto
your
living
room floor

Now you can go
and collect all those
letters and string them
back together to duplicate
these sentences or you can
use that same pile of letters
to continue writing a better
version of your story one
that puts you back on
track to awakening
the witnessing
awareness
of your
soul

The
choice is
entirely yours

Wordless awareness is the unifying thread
woven into this crazy tapestry of words

The only way to truly understand
this mystery is to sink into the
formless depths of your
own consciousness
by gazing into
the space
inside
your
head
and once
you've sunken
all the way down
into the groundless
ground of being God
will rise up from those
bottomless depths to
send you back home
where your higher
self exists in an
infinite realm
of spiritual bliss
and consciousness

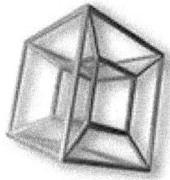

Everything written in the book of your life
is erased from the pages once you
dip your soul in the invisible
elixir of infinity where
we all take root
and grow
like
acorns
into massive
oak trees roused
by the mystical winds
moving through this world
animating each form flowing
from God's formless mystery

Everything within
existence is energy in
one formation or another
for all the forms and forces
in creation come from the
same formless dimension

Strings of energy weave
reality together all so
our sleeping souls
can reawaken
while living
in our tender
skins on this precious
blue jewel of a planet twirling
through a macrocosm of realms
made of dreams forming each place
in mercurial space on different planes
of existence from pure consciousness

Reading this grimoire can feel like watching
circles continuously drawn on scores of
these pages except that the circles
are all made out of words and
the paper is a palimpsest

Keep gazing upon
and grazing on
these daisy
chains
full
of
ones
and zeros
and after all the
dominoes of thought
fall a garland of wordless
awareness crowns your head
as you drift into headlessness

Whenever your consciousness is
at one with life you feel the
same energy that gives
rise to everything in
creation is also
vibrating at
the very
core of
your being
and that's when
the still small voice in
your soul starts whispering
stuff like everything is going to
be okay don't go back to sleep and
keep trying to become a better person

Such vast yet equally
small portions of
eternity seep
into and
out of
all
my
words
no matter
what they say

Place your hand on
any page of this book
to release some of this
immortal elixir into your
current state of being

Close your eyes
and focus on
soaking
up
all the
energy you
need to turn back
into the bliss of infinity

A
mind
caught in
words and
thoughts
can't be
free
so
what
words shall
I put inside your
head to remove the
thoughts these words
wind up putting in there?

When you reach the end
of this message focus
all your attention
solely on the
full stop
staying
perfectly
still till your
mind is muted .

The letters printed in this
book might look like
ordinary letters
but they're
actually
slits
in
the
fabric
of creation
your soul keeps
slipping into God's
magnificence through

Stay here for a moment
and revel in the level of
being with me before
you leave this page
then keep reading
my poetry for
joy grows
in the hearts
of those who rest in
awareness without thinking

How
long shall I
continue sending
out these signals from
the bottomless depths of
being bubbling to the outer
surface where all things exist?

I just said it but I'll say it again

From a formless oneness this
cosmos came creating all of
reality which is unified by
a groundless ground
found by plunging
inwardly that
lifts you
up
into the
transcendent
source of creation

All of the
words in this book
work in concert like an
array of directional lenses
perpetually resolving your
vision into a cosmic view
unifying everything you
can experience and
because of the
algorithm
used to
place
this
text
on the
page you
can also see
a steady pattern
pointing you in and
down and up and out to
reach your measureless self

I keep talking about going in and
down and up and out to get
you back to the place
where everything
is unified by
nothing
but
b
e
i
n
g

If you
make the
mirror of your
soul like a window
you'll see everything in
reality from the formlessness
of infinity as easily as closing your
eyes before opening them again slowly

An interesting
thing about this book
is that if you were to rip out
all the pages and tear them up
into fragments then scattered all
of those pieces of paper across
your living room floor and then
started putting together odd
combinations of those torn
out sections and reading
them you'd still get a
sense of the unity
within diversity
woven into
the fabric
of time &
space from
the inky realm
of infinity writing a
book with fractals too

As long as you keep turning these pages I'll
keep spilling ink for your soul to sink into
the iridescent blackness of God through

Remember these words are portals

Recall the blank page analogy

This book you are holding

The room you are in

Your awareness

Everything
comes
from
the
same
invisible
primordial
and mercurial
medium all things
come into being from

These words erase me
when they come
through me
and the
hands
that wrote
them also left a
long time ago now

Emptiness is where I live

Where are you right now? Are
you with me as your awareness
ever aware of itself via the feed
back loop to and from infinity?

If so you already know what
a thrill it is crossing paths
with other invisible fish
swimming in the sea
of tranquility up
here on the
moon all
day & night

Would you like me to stop
rhyming off riddles to
help you solve the
puzzle of reality
once and for all?

This is a subject that
never ends unless you
see you are the subject

Stop chasing words to
make separate objects
become one because
enlightenment won't
ever stick that way

To truly transcend
duality you've got to
plumb pure subjectivity

Most people stay in the shallowest
depths of being and emptiness
when it's time for dipping in
the ocean of God but us
liberated souls simply
stop holding back
and drown into
the void fully

There's also
an ongoing
conversation
among us seers
who read and write
mystical prose & poetry
about how reality is actually
like a painting on a palimpsest
or a formless field full of ephemeral
forms alive via immaculate conception

I once wrote a short poem on a postcard
that I bought on vacation and sent it
to a friend celebrating the fierce
light at the heart of creation

It was a real grinder
of a poem all
about the
miracle
of star
factories
burning off
plasma to create
stardust so we can make
beauty from ashes like God does

Sometimes the ungraspable
vastness of pure being
wells up inside my
heart so fast it
starts racing
like a bird
freed from
a cage flying
to catch up with
the surge of ecstasy
and sometimes giant
flocks take flight that
sculpt these lovely
shapes of divine
rapture in my
head after
I'm startled
awake by the
immensity of God

Sometimes a surge of bliss
makes your spirit soar
out of your chest
but normally
you have
to go
way
down
into the
neverending
ground of being
before your soul can
fly back up to God again

Throw a rope into the abyss and
slowly lower yourself down then climb
a ladder high into the sky & kick it away

There are other ways you
can visualize your way
back to God that are
as easy as child's play
you can picture diving off
a cliff into a bottomless lake
or floating in a shoreless sea
that goes on eternally or see
yourself sinking like a stone
into the unending ocean all
so your spirit can rise up
above your head and
make you feel just
like a marionette
dancing on waves
of bliss & tripping the
light fantastic through air

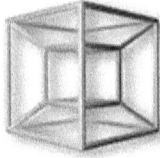

Every
now and then
an unseen hand will
edit these poems when
I step away from the screen

The same hand has even made
money materialize in my bank
account which sounds crazy
but these sorts of things
happen to me all
the time
now

On
a fairly
average day
entire sentences
just like these ones will
appear in my head waiting to
be written down by my willing hands

I couldn't keep up with all the inspired words
and phrases clamoring inside me today
wanting to fly out of my original face
like starlings winging ecstatically
and darting every which way
without losing cohesion
in a startling display
of murmuration

The sheer size of it
all made my soul kneel
like a statue and just listen

Silence is the first language
of God and the mother
tongue of the soul

Silence is the
essence
of our
souls
and
the
best
route to
enlightenment

Silence is a solvent
that dissolves the ego
and enlarges the soul

Silence is a portal
to the limitless
ocean of
being
and the
soundtrack
of true liberation

Listen to the fertile ground
of silence until it grows
beyond all bounds
and sounds

Thinking
of things blinds
us to the miracle of
the world we're living in

Even the idea of a lotus flower
can hide the blossoming of this
beautiful form of formlessness

See how everything arises
from silence and keeps
emerging from it

One thing
and then another
and then something else

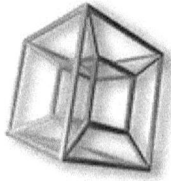

Our
world is
an oracle of
divine displays

Watch the dawn mist
glowing as the morning
sun rises over a dewy field

Rest your gaze on the blue sky
just above the horizon to travel
beyond the clouds of thought
occupying your monkey mind

Take a tranquil walk along
the beach and let the
sighs of the waves
lapping on the
shore remind you
of the eternal ocean
of all being & becoming

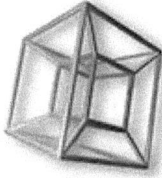

Take your shoes off and
stand on the earth
barefoot until
your feet
remember
what your head
is always forgetting

Your body was born in
the world but your soul
comes from a mystery
beyond the blue sky

Dig the roots of
your toes into
the ground
and wait
for the
lotus
flower's
revelation to
blossom from the
lake inside your eyes

I was just about to share some
more mystical insights but
something suddenly
came up out of
nowhere so
would you
mind holding on
for just a sec? I'll be
right back to share my
next message with you

Don't let the hoax of time
steal your patience while
I'm gone and remember
that your soul thrives
on mystery even
more than it
does on certainty

Okay I'm back now so where were we
again? Oh yes you were ideally waiting
for me in the present moment and I was
about to tell you how the alchemy of your
heart and mind are like the sun and moon

We're getting into something really cool
again that I can't explain any other way

God manifested our universe by
transmuting dark energy into
matter so carbon could
bond with untold
atoms to form
the molecules
needed to create
the myriad creatures
and ten thousand things

This next part can be a
bit hard to believe
your first time
hearing
it

Our
nearby
golden sun
that makes life
thrive on earth was
choreographed by God
to cross the sky as a beacon
of the loving brilliance pulsating
in an awakened heart and the moon
that generates the tides of life is a signal
for the serene glow of the enlightened mind

Don't dismiss the sun and moon
as objects of meditation or
as spiritual symbols for
the blazing sun is
so glorious
that the
vivid
moon
holds vigil
every night to
take delight in this
exquisite light shining
in the firmament and we
also wax and wane like the
moon & can shine as bright
as the sun at noon once we
let infinity balloon inside us

You
already
have a heart
of gold as well as
a mirror in your head
that you'll need to be a
liberated human being
so don't let your loving
or looking become too
dim or dull or shady or
when it does gaze at
reality like a glassy
lake at night and
eventually your
whole being
will sparkle
and shine
like dappling
sunlight on waves
of transcendental bliss
and nondual knowingness

When's the last time
you got up early
to watch the
sunrise or
better
yet
stayed up
the whole night
in a field somewhere
watching the moon and
the clouds and the stars
all roam across the vault
of heaven waiting for the
sun to come up? Don't
leave this world until
you've done that
at least once in
this brief but
long-lasting life
that continues on in
the astral plane after life

So you know the whole
sky is a skry made
for us to get
mystical
on

When
we stare
at it for long
spells it shows us
all its hidden secrets

Not just the sun & moon but
all that space between the stars
and also black holes & quasars are
all oracles about our true nature and the
luminous and spacious true nature of reality

Your soul
contains a dazzling
spark of intelligent bliss
as brilliant and smart as any
one of the numberless stars
& you're a jewel-eyed marvel
with the power to connect
whole constellations of
thought and grok
galaxies
of connectivity
and ultimately know the
oneness of everything in reality

You
must have
heard it before
or somehow knew
that our lovely moon
is like a magnet made
to lift our souls up and
out onto a higher plane
beyond our earthly one

Gaze upon it and it'll
effortlessly transport
you into the same
ascended light
reflecting
state
of pure
awareness
plus a syzygy
with the inner sun
can also happen that
sends us straight into the
light at the heart of creation

Meditate on
the mesmerizing
power of the moon
until its illuminating
glow magnetically
elevates the eye
of your soul

And learn to
see the wisdom
in the lunar cycle

How it grows like a
seed that blooms
and dies then
repeats the
process
showing
us the circle
of life and death
and reincarnation that
God uses to keep our lives
and everything in creation going

After being moonlike by
witnessing the world
focus on the inner
sun by gazing
deeply into
the dark
screen
behind your
closed eyes and let
the photons dancing on
the back of your eyelids pull
you into the cosmic light at the
heart of creation then stay there
as long as you can bear it before
dividing and diving back in again

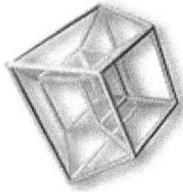

The space between the stars is
made of consciousness and
awakening feels just like
entering a black hole
that takes you back
into a singularity
at the heart of
everything
in reality
and this
dying before
we die lights us up
like quasars in a night sky
where most souls wander like far
away stars searching for a nearby God

Your
soul is as
vast as the sky
and the miracle of
your awareness arises
seemingly out of the blue

All that happens in this world
comes and goes like the clouds
and thoughts and feelings pass
through us all like the weather

All this wisdom is in you

It is your birthright
for being born
in a human
body

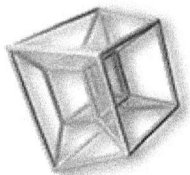

An awake soul won't cast
unconscious shadows

It's a lot more
like being a
full moon on
a cloudless day

A translucent lens
that always sees the
world inside a circle
that's one with the
dazzling source
of creation
beyond the
endless blue sky
of the liberated mind's
highest abode in heaven

Learn to ascend the way
water turns to vapor
and becomes a
passing cloud
that disappears
then ride a thermal
of witnessing for a while
until you shine like the sun
and glow like the moon then
bask in the firmament as the
sparkling awareness you are
before lighting out in the
darkness of infinity for
another visit to see
and feel the oneness
of everything in existence
forming from formless energy

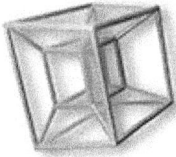

Once
upon a time
when the stars
were much closer
together only the
light of creation
was seen but
since then
the light
spread out
all so specks
like us can look
up in wonderment

Remember when I said
the sky holds secrets? This
one is about how more love is
always gained by giving it away

When you live
under the
light
of
your
higher self
all kinds of highly
evolved beings hang
around your opening
sending down holy
energies to help
you move
forward
on your
spiritual
pilgrimage

Assistance from
the angelic realm is
another boon of living
in the awakened state
of being one with God
and everything there is

I'll often tweak spiritual techniques
to make them better or easier

An extremely powerful
modified practice
is sungazing
which is
commonly
done with your
eyes open at dusk
or dawn to minimize
the risk of vision loss

Sungazing with your
eyes closed is way
safer and can be
done any time
you can see
a full sun

What
you do next
is difficult but key

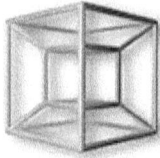

Close your eyes
and gaze at
the sun
with
your
third eye
and watch as
the light fills your
head first followed by
your body before it flows
into your auric energy field

Let this luminous energy lift your
spirit so high it soars to the summit
of ecstasy then tilt your head back so
even more of this brilliant bliss pours in

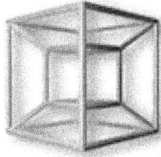

When you close your eyes
the darkness you see is
manifesting reality
and when you
open your
eyes all
that you
can see and
touch and feel is
God's light giving form
to that formless mystery and
from the awakened state of being
you can make the universe disappear
and reappear simply by blinking slowly
as pure consciousness anytime you want
to bring this immaculate perception back

There
already exists
a singularity that
will take you back
to infinity unifying
everything and
everyone in
reality
so
if you
are finally
ready to explore
this mystical portal it is
found by looking within and
seeing how God is an eternal
being made of formless energy
a portion of which you embody
as a boundless soul living in a
human body with an earnest
heart and a headless head

While writing this book
I dreamt I was taking
a closeup picture
of the moon
with my
third
eye
like a
telescope

Spiritual messages
kept flashing on this digital
billboard by the sea of tranquility
which made their way into this book

This dream also means my words are like
a magnifying lens you can zoom in and out
through revealing the mystery hidden within
you that takes you back to your original face
gazing out from infinity like a fishing moon

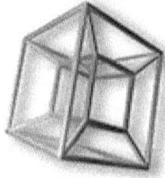

Cast all your troubles and concerns away and
go fishing for some of God's grace today

Who knows? You might get lucky

This could be the day you
throw your line in and
finally catch the
moon once
and for
all

Then
seekers may
start to drift near
you secretly hoping
to get a lift whenever
you decide to witness
the world go by from
that transcendental
state of spiritual
illumination

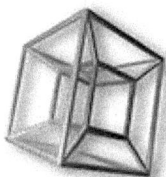

Just as
a full moon
can appear in
the reflection
of a small
pool
so
too
can the
formless face
of infinity fit inside
your not so finite head

The truth is we're all looking
out at these holographic vistas
of reality with the eyes of God

We just keep on forgetting to
watch the world go by while
witnessing to make room
for our view to loom as
high and wide as
the moon

When soulmates find each other
it's like the ocean meeting
the shore or the earth
and sky uniting on
the horizon to
make the
two as
one

A
union
to couple
your soul with
God is also ready
to happen inside you

Behind your shimmering eyes
the swell of infinity yearns for you
to come home so the ground of your
being can fly into the sky & fuse with it

Here's
a special note
if you're ever feeling
a bit spiritually homeless

We are never as close to God
as we are when we're all alone

Just beyond your tunnel vision
the awakened gaze of your
slumbering soul is just
waiting to shine
like a full
moon
on a quiet
cloudless night

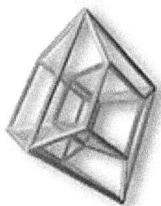

Deep inside my soul I know
you are a wondrous being
full of hopes and dreams
but maybe you've lost
your way a bit lately

Whenever I'm
bummed
out my
soul begins
singing the lyrics
from a Rolling Stones
song which goes you can't
always get what you want but
if you try sometimes well you just
might find you get what you need

Do all of those scriptures
you heard about God
exacting revenge
and smiting
sinners
for
bad
behavior
seem silly now
that you're grown up?

Do you really think the Creator
of the Universe is unwilling to spank us
on occasion? Newsflash! Think again kiddos

Sharp pebbles kept getting stuck
in my shoes today and fire
ants were biting me
in all my tender
spots after
a bunch
of my unruly
neighbors all came
by earlier on looking to
rub shoulders with me and
grab a bit of free advice to feel
better but what does this have to
do with you? I'll fill you in one day if
we ever get close and I ever need to

Quit
all of your
moaning and
groaning over shit
that isn't the problem

All those wounds you're
carrying around inside
you are pathways
to something
better &
freer

If you'll
stop pushing
the hurt away and
feel your emotional pain
healing and clarity will emerge
from the inner depths of your being

One of the
worst fates is to
become a shit talker
serving up bullshit and
lies with other assholes

You might as well cram
actual crap right down
each other's throats
as a really potent
remedy since
you won't
eat your
own shorts

The truth about
love or hate is that
the more you give the
more you always get back

Of all the paths we can follow in life there is
one that matters more than anything else

It is the path of a true human being

The beautiful ones who are
always spreading love
and positivity and
bringing out
the best
in all
the
lost or
sleeping souls
still wandering around
this world wondering how to
get back to a home we never left

Part of the joy of living comes from
what we tell ourselves whenever
something happens to us but
the bulk of it comes from
resting in the spiritual
essence of our souls

Every slight starts out
small and grows bigger
when we fixate on it so
choose your thoughts
wisely to shift your
self talk into
making
your
way through
life more gracefully

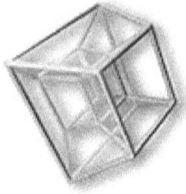

All
these
drops of
knowledge
are meant to
baptize your
mind using
purifying
words
so
you
won't
be afraid
of drowning
and being born
again from the ocean
of being where your soul's
awareness arises from the same
emptiness upon which all things depend

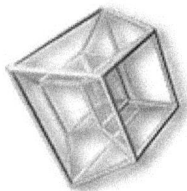

The boundless dimension of your soul
can only be known by experiencing it
so let's go there right now you and
I and breathe in that rarefied air

Take your shoes & socks
off and tune into the
heartbeat of life
thrumming
beneath
the soles
of your feet

Let yourself become
one with the groundless
ground of being at the heart
of reality until you feel the whole
world vibrating from the vibrant bliss
of knowing the emptiness of existence

Karma isn't just a force
that compels us to
speak and feel
and act the
way we
do

All
of it is
also always
subtly spawning
our karmic struggles
so our souls can mature

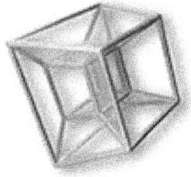

Thoughts shape our attitudes
which color the emotional
lens for the films inside
our televising heads

Don't let this
world rob
the joy
that
comes
from feeling
the bliss of being
completely imageless
remember we're all just
portions of infinity living in
our mortal shells so cherish
the gift of life you've been
given and keep spreading
as much loving energy
as you can summon
and share every
single day
as there
really is no
better way to live
on any plane of existence

| WHATEVER WILL BE WILL BE | SO SHALL IT BE |

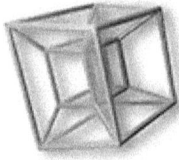

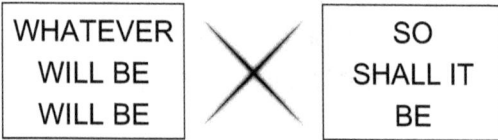

Another two skeleton keys
our souls came here to
loyally live by in this
royal incarnation
we're born into

We are also here to
exist with each other in
peace and harmony and
evolve as spiritual beings
who will one day shape
and surf the waves of
our shared reality
with the same
fluency we feel in
those states of flow we
find and follow individually

So
now that
you know what
it takes to remember
the endless field of infinity
all these words keep pointing to
don't wait outside yourself any longer
go inside and shut the door behind you
& close your eyes & sit still until your
thoughts & feelings calm down so
much they're gone and then let
yourself sink into the silent
depths of pure being
rising up from a
groundless
ground
that
sends
your soul
soaring above
the mountains after
passing through the valley
of shadows and your ego's death

Every spiritual seeker has
to go through a dark
night of the soul
or two or
maybe
even three
or four or more
before becoming a
totally liberated human

It's part of the purification
process that prepares your
body and heart and mind
for all the plunging and
rising into the cosmic
mystery of being

We can't
incarnate
the glory of
our higher selves
until we drop our egos
& conquer our lower selves

Absolute nothingness as far
as the third eye can see
is necessary to find
the freedom of
God in our
spiritual
core
right before
diving all the way
in so your soul can
swim out beyond all
thoughts to become
one with the eternal
ocean of your true
self & then rest
in the simple
feeling of
being until you
start soaking up the
liberating oneness of life
witnessing everything spring
into existence from a primordial
source we're all already one with

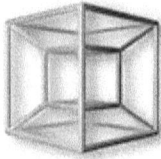

Go beyond all
words and
ways of
thinking
about the
absolute truth

Silence is by far the
best way to become
totally one with God

We have to stay as
still as statues to
see that who
we are is a
portion
of infinity
inhabiting a
human body in
this physical dream
we experience as reality

Life is a balancing act
between letting go
and holding on
but we have
to let go
of form
before
we can
embody
the fullness
of formlessness
and fully fathom the
yabyum of nondual being

Are you still too attached to life?
If so gaze into the middle distance
until there's nothing left but being

Our souls are on
a feedback loop with
the source of existence
while moving through
this world of form

Ultimately there's only the eternal now
and our beings which are made to
sparkle and shine with divine
bliss by embodying the
cosmic light of
creation
and the
original realm
of formlessness that
existed before the big bang

If you expand into the ocean of being
enough times you'll eventually
stop contracting and settle
into what you always
already are as
your true
self

A
nondual
field of sensing
awareness in a wider
field of awareness floating
down the dreamy river of time
knowing that consciousness is the
origin and essence of everything in
this or any other realm of existence

Laugh a lot. Cry when you feel sad. Show kindness when it's needed. Be helpful. Don't blame others when you're the one responsible. Live honestly. Stop comparing yourself to others. Love yourself. Run your own race. Be real. Listen closely. Share with others. Any other tidbits of wisdom that you need to recall right now?

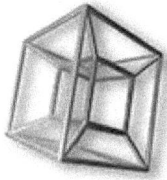

A Spiritual Rx with unlimited refills

Take all your worries & concerns
and hold them inside the hollow
space created when you inhale
and when you exhale release
all that tension and worry
adding a long deep
sigh whenever
necessary

Repeat a
minimum of
three times a day
for the next few weeks

Continue using as often as needed

Forget about the part
of you that keeps
getting lost in
form for a
minute
as you
focus on
the formless
dimension within

On the flip side of
life all the outlines
separating things
begin blurring as
every face and
form slowly
dissolves
into the
invisible &
mercurial dark
energy of infinity
manifesting reality in
such vivid & varied ways

All
forms are
forms of formless
energy and life is made
up of errands and routines

Each day has its own patterns

Learn to take a moment or two
or three or four or more each
day to be less concerned
with the outer surface
of form and more
attuned to the
formless source
giving rise to it all

Through the simple magic
of ink and paper your
soul and my soul
keep getting
liberated in
tandem by all
the printed words
on these white pages

I'm sure we'll keep on meeting
like this in all kinds of wonderful
and completely unexpected ways

Here hop on this raft with me right
now and let's paddle to the other
shore together for a quick visit
and hopefully we'll have the
wind at our backs along
with the moon on our
stern as we whisk
our way back to
that place we all
come from before we
are born into this world of
living and dying formless form

The difference between reading
about the awakened state
and awakening is a
journey that
can take a lot
of different lifetimes
but final enlightenment
can also happen right now
because you already are the
luminous awareness you seek
that kindles stars in your eyes
alights the moon in your head
and sets the sun in your chest

It just keeps getting eclipsed
by all the thoughts you have
floating around inside your
mind looking for the one
answer that will end
your search for
something
you've
never really
forgotten nor fully
grokked once and for all

When your mind is racing
and a bunch of random
thoughts are whizzing
through your head
like chainsaws
try letting
them
pass
by like
rumbling
trains far off
in the distance at
night and you'll swiftly
discover that all the hustle
and bustle of living is actually
a gateway to the eternally quiet
hush beneath every surface rush

After the passing trains of thought
have come and gone and the
dust from doing finally
settles you're left
with nothing
but the
empty
presence
of your being
and an awareness
of the recurring moment

If you fall in love with the formless
essence generating this timeless state
of consciousness you'll free yourself easily
and begin to unleash the power within us to
transform this world into a heavenly paradise

You
gotta try
this ancient
alchemical trick
for getting rid of any
mental chatter cluttering
the tabula rasa in your head

Start by visualizing writing out all
your unwanted thoughts on a sheet
of paper hovering against a blue sky
then picture setting that page on fire
and watching it burn into ashes as a
gust of wind blows the dust away
dissolving all your thoughts and
your emotional attachments
to them as they disappear
into thin air like a fine
powder and letting
your ego go along
for the ride into the
freedom of emptiness

A
newer
version of
this method is
to visualize typing
out strings of thoughts
on a computer screen then
hitting the delete button to get
rid of them along with your ego by
dissolving those electric bits of data in
to the blackness beyond the white page

Since we're on the topic of computers now
I'd like to take this opportunity to update the
blank page analogy to include digital screens
if you look closely at the white background on
a new document you will see these tiny color
teenies propagating the virtual blank page
and if you stare at it long enough you'll
start seeing those same vibrating
particles of light forming tiny
yet fleeting luminous
strings of energy
secretly weaving the
rest of reality together like
a pixelated fabricated fantasy

How long's it been since you
pierced the veil of reality
and gazed into the
formless field of
energy your
original
face is from?

Let's get you back
to where you belong

The amazing state of
absolute emptiness
is a realm beyond
language so no
more words
for now

Only
silence &
looking within
will take you back
to where there is here
& make the two one again

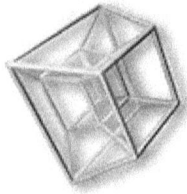

It's time to light this frayed
rope on fire again and
give my words an
unforgettable
hot new
whirl

Maybe
I'll spin them
over my head today
or fashion a lasso for you to
do a flaming hoop dance through

All this wordplay just to remind you of the
stillness at the center of your being that lives
on after each new circle of life begins & ends

My words are also like windblown leaves
falling from the tree of immortality and
twirling around the original ground
of your being like silhouettes
doing pirouettes before
disappearing while
taking your ego
with them and
they also like
digging down
into your depths
like roots with shoots
that send your soul soaring
above the swaying treetops into
the blue sky of your liberated mind
before dissolving into pure emptiness

Our
divine souls
are made to soar
with angelic wings on
an exquisitely delicate
ecstasy yet we often fly
around like misguided
moths worshiping the
spiritless light from
street lamps at
midnight
when deep
within what we
are really yearning
for is the mesmerizing
glow of moonlit eyes & the
kamikaze kiss of dying in flames

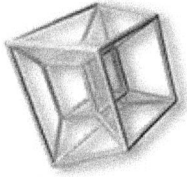

You don't need
very much
to enjoy
the bliss
of knowingness

Access to some nearby
woods and the writings of
your favorite writers and any
holy books you find inspiring
then time to read and reflect
as you sit or stand then walk
while staring fluently into
the emptiness of space
so the yoking gaze
of oneness can
fill you up so
much it goes on
for nights and days

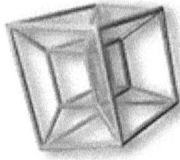

If
you
want to
explore the
mystical side of
life spend an hour or
so every day sauntering in
nature getting centered before
winding your way back home and
you'll start seeing and hearing how
everything speaks to you once you
stop to have a look and just listen
to the wind and the trees and the
rivers and all the creatures on
the land and in the sky and
in the sea that all have
something to share
about the truth
of God and
you and
reality

When tall grasses sway & swirl
in the wind doing tai chi
or trees bend and
bow yogically
overhead
who'd
ever
deny
feeling
a mystical
energy flowing
through the air? We
evolved in forests and fields
and spending time in them naturally
returns us to our roots as spiritual beings

Walking in nature
is a simple and
easy way to
awaken
the
presence
of pure being

You just need to pause
every now and zen to truly
appreciate how every single
thing is actually living energy

Listening to the wispy breeze
blowing through the leaves
while focusing on the joy
of breathing also stirs
your soul's sense
of the invisible
forces of nature
animating all of life
without which we would
not be alive for a nanosecond

You've
probably heard
the analogy of the two
birds clinging to the same tree

One eats fruit and the other looks on

The bird eating is your body involved
in life and the bird watching is your
soul beholding all of it unfolding

We gain experience in
the world of form
but we know
and grow
because
our souls
can figure
things out by
contemplating the
meaning of anything we
can experience in this world
or any of the others in existence

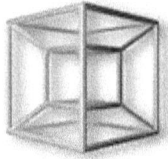

Most people prefer being the bird
flitting about here and there
far more than the one
who just sits and
watches but
we need
both
to
live
from
egoless
awareness

Why do you think
spiritual people spend
time sitting in meditation?

So that the liberated state of
being is also available during
the doing every day of living

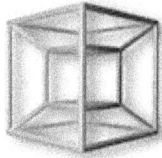

Sit in meditation like the
birds after they've
flown around
having fun
finding
food
and
finally
finished
singing a few
more lovely tunes

Spend some time every day
observing life's passing scenes like
the deer in the woods gazing out at the
world while grazing and foraging for food

We've forgotten how important it is to watch
the world go by with wordless awareness the
same way all of God's other offspring still do

When
we can't see
the forest from the
trees it means we're too
close to a situation and need to
step back to gain some perspective

A half an inch just behind your face is all
you need to sink into transcendent space

When this zooming in and out is working
properly we're fully present and taking
care of the correct task at hand with
one foot in this world and one in
the formless witnessing life's
drama unfolding with a
sense of humor and
a healthy dose
of serenity
to enjoy
the play
of it all with
total equanimity

It's the crow's caw I often mimic
with these inspired footprints
scrawled across the page
crying out Wake up!
Wake up! Wake
up! Wake
up!

And
not just the
crows I've heard
other birds sharing
mystical secrets too
the owl's sublime hu
is the most uplifting
mantra that we can
chant and there's
also the hawk's
screech saying
let your spirit soar
and who can forget the
honking geese flying in delta
formation pointing the way home

Caw like a crow
to call more
awareness
into your
life then
meditate
like an owl
chanting the
mystical syllable
hu until your spirit
soars like an eagle
seeing things from
your higher self's
bird's-eye view
and keep it
up until
you're
living on
the banks of
being like a mink
slipping into and out
of the unseen without
even needing to blink

Have you heard the story about
the two young fish? They're
swimming along and
meet an older fish
swimming the
other way
who nods
at them and says
Morning boys! How's
the water? The two younger
fish swim on for a bit until one
of them looks over at the other
and says what the hell is water?

Have you already figured out the
actual gist of the two young fish
who don't know what water is?
The older fish knows the real
nature of reality we live in

Water is a metaphor
for consciousness
a mercurial medium
all the forms & forces in
creation flow into form from

The way clouds send down raindrops covering
everything in shimmering beads of wetness
or the way a river wends its way through
reality or the perpetual motion of the
waves lapping on the shores or the
swelling of the oceans & seas
are all living testimonies of
the absolute truth that
we are all a part of
the ongoing stream
of life and forever one
with the source of creation
manifesting everything into form
from the formless dimension of being

So much divine nature that
we are born with gets
buried under ruins
left in the past
by our egos
as stories held
in branches that
are made from the
tree of life break off
and fall into new and
old piles but beneath
all our broken dreams
and unfulfilled desires
we're all still waves in
the ocean walking on
water like Jesus did
who knew as fully
as anyone else
before him
or since
that life is
but a game
by God made
for us to sink and
swim and soar within

We
have to
devour our
tales like the
ouroboros does

This deadly elliptical
symbol first originated
in ancient Egypt and was
adopted by the alchemists

It captures the paradox of the
path to enlightenment ending
at the same place as it begins
and also signifies the death
or dissolution of the ego
required to free our
souls from the
stories in our
mortal shells
and our coiled
sheaths or koshas

Like the ouroboros
we have to eat
our egos
like a
serpent
swallowing
its own tail until
there's nothing left
but the emptiness of
pure consciousness

That's when your
body is shed
and your
soul's
essence
reconnects
with the formless
dimension once again

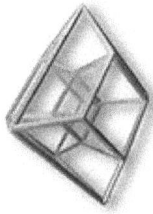

To
reveal
the naked
essence of our
original nature we
have to burrow into
the depths of our
being to uncoil
the snake that
sheds our skin
after offering us
fruit from the tree
of God's immortality

Beneath these fleshy forms
is an immaculate conception
born without a beginning that
goes on forever as the energy
of being authoring everything

Learn to live upstream
before your thoughts
flow down through
channels carved
into your own
groundless
ground of
being by
the grooves
playing on rerun
in your talking head
by watching them pass
then float away like leaves
falling into a moving river to
remember how much simpler
life is when not fixed or frozen
by our sticky and clingy egos

Meditation without introspection is like
dozing off for a brief spell when we
are meant to meet our Maker

Connecting with the
fullness of the
formless
realm
involves
following the
correct procedure

The initial phase of sitting is
best spent organizing your outer
life and doing any inner work so you
can get into the second phase of sitting
which is all about emptying your mind
so you can start gazing into the
formless essence of your
consciousness and
plunging into
the bottomless
void of it so God
can lift you up into
the shaded sanctuary
where we all come from

Close your eyes and follow your breath
until your mind stops wandering
and your breathing slows
down considerably

Once you are
calm focus
on being
still like
a statue

This includes
all the glissades &
saccades our eyes make

Once your body's locked in a trance
your mind slowly shifts into a static yet
highly alert state of looking which is the
eternal observer in you and the gateway
to the inner freedom of your true nature

Inquire into the source of witnessing to
bypass Ramana's extra step of seeing
the unreality of the I-thought first to
fly even faster to your higher self

A popular definition for living
enlightenment in Zen is
before awakening
chop wood
carry water
after awakening
chop wood carry water

The basic idea is to use daily
chores as an opportunity to be
fully present to the task at hand
while purifying or removing any
unresolved stuff that may arise

So for instance when cleaning
windows you appreciate the
physical pleasure of this
activity while wiping
away the fetters
from living
and you
also do the
same sweeping
the floors or washing
dishes or any other chores

This
next story
is from a crazy
news report about
this squirrel that was
ambushing people from
a tree above the sidewalk

The locals suspected rabies

Turns out the little critter just
wanted pedestrians to walk
around his property and
not traipse right into
his living room

Moral of this story?

Make sure you get enough
alone time without anyone else
around to disturb you and your zen

I used to think that the old
lady who talks to birds
was as nutty as the
squirrels but now
that we are a lot
more alike this way
I bet that bird lady also
enjoys looking at faces in
natural features in a game
of peek-a-boo the world still
likes playing with us to lift
our moods and push us
through any remaining
or lingering fears or
unfinished issues
so we can return
to the emptiness
of being a lens for
God to gaze through

I'm not a
very big guy but
it's possible one day
I'll be weighed-in as one
of the heavyweight gurus

God-intoxicating joy and the
incredible freedom of being
still lightens my load and
puts a sweet spring in
my step but the
gravity of
God-realization
also makes me feel
as sober and serious &
heavy as stone sometimes

Everyone's inside me now
and my tendency is to
pick things apart
so every few
days or
so
I
take
a really
long walk
in the woods
to get away from
people or I turn into
a boulder rolling around
pulverizing all the big egos
running roughshod in my hood

I
can't
seem to
stop penning
these poems now
they flow through me
every time I go out for a
stroll in the woods where
I'll wind up downloading
yet another reminder of
your witnessing soul
watching as you're
reading these
words or
some other
spiritual truth by
revealing it poetically

Today I saw three dragonflies
dancing in the air together while
tracing some of God's thoughts with
their flight paths first forming a vortex
then a double helix before finishing off
with a complex arabesque full of flair

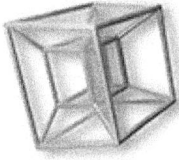

Cool stuff happens
when your soul
stays open
like how
way up
above like
clockwork the
exact same hawk
returned for a third
week in a row and
called out to me
in recognition
of my lofty
state as I
entered the
woods for my
Sunday morning
walk and dogs are
continually breaking
away from their owners
to come over and bask in
the rainbow of enlightening
energies flashing around inside
the atmosphere of my loving aura

I once negotiated
splitting a caramel in half
with a squirrel who climbed up
onto my chest and demanded some
of the candy I had just put in my mouth
and the next day I was mobbed by a flock
of pigeons in a park to satisfy a doubting
Thomas who witnessed my crazy squirrel
exchange that occurred the day before

The truth is I live in a sublime state
of communion with the natural
world now and no I haven't
lost my mind I still have
the gift of gab and
I'm continuously
rubbing shoulders
with folks seeking more
love but I prefer spending time
alone or with people who are comfortable
leaving room for silence to enter the conversation

Deep
in the woods
a lone wolf howls
signaling the coming
of night and as the sun
goes down the animals
know it's still game on

Many hide and get on
guard for prowlers
while hunters go
into stealth
mode

Whether
predator or prey
all of God's creatures
big & small worship the
mystery of life at the heart
of the give and take in this
living world we all call home

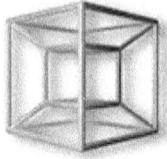

On
my walk
today I came
upon a strange
looking spider I
had not seen
before and
when I
stooped
for a closer
look it magically
vanished into thin air

Supernatural proof that God
manifests the web of life from the
formless dimension and will make stuff
appear and disappear to show us this truth

A
direct
line from
God just sent
me this message

You are the web and the
weaver and the watcher and
the prey in the invisible mandala
creating your silky and sticky reality

You are beyond divisions of this or that

Someone who knows there can't be an
is without an isn't or a world of form
without the formless dimension

Now open your third eye
and see for yourself
that it's all just a
dream in one
universal
mind
of
I
AM

I'm still speaking on behalf of God who
asked me to send you this message

What you call awareness is
a lens I made to know
myself through
you and
what
you
think of
as your life
is nothing more
than a passing breeze

A pattern of being echoing
through the world that leaves
a trace but is inherently empty

You've heard it said you're like a
wave in the ocean but it feels more
like being the whole ocean in a wave

Or you've been told you're like a fish
swimming in the sea but it feels
more like the entire sea is
swimming in the fish

It's that deep
knowing
down
inside
your soul
that it's all just
one massive swaying
ocean of neverending being

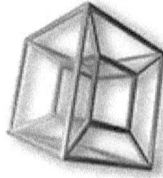

We are nearing the end of this book now
so any remaining entries still to come
will be the last ones I'm going to
share with you before I head
back inside this invisible
box of consciousness
I've been blessed
with for more
or less my
entire
life

It's
been a
titanic treat
playing the poet
and putting together
images with you to reveal
the riches & treasures buried
deep within the ocean of your soul

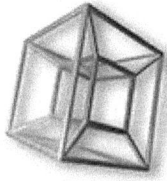

There aren't any through-and-through
or out-and-out goodbyes because
ultimately we are not separate

It's also possible for us
to connect on the
subtle planes
where our
souls
can
roam
more freely

So maybe we'll meet
somewhere up there among
the stars where all our dreams and
astral travels and in-between lives occur
or if you try summoning me when you need
some guidance I might visit you in your sleep
or simply pop in your head with a liberating tip

There's no limit to the number of lives
we can live because we don't really
die we keep moving from one
incarnation to the next like
shifting scenes in an
ongoing story
that gets
way
more
enjoyable
once we reach
the climax of creation
and live as awakened beings
on an adventure of consciousness
through all worlds and planes of reality

What is time but slices
of life streaming by
so seamlessly we
don't see that
the tubular
way we
wend
our
way
through
reality are all
shifting scenes in
one eternal moment
flashing on and off like a
fleeting stroboscopic show

Whatever view you use to unravel
this ancient enigma I'm just glad that
we've been able to spend this much of
our time together seeing through being

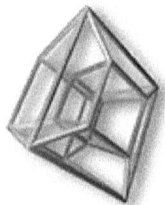

It's possible we've known each other
in past lives but even if that's
not the case we are all
unified by the
mystery
of
b
e
i
n
g

Turn your attention
inward right now and allow
the swell of silence to lift your soul
into the formless dimension manifesting
everything into existence every single second

Call
me crazy
all you want
but my karma is
loving humanity so
much it pains my soul

Now don't get me wrong

There is an immense amount
of joy in knowing you are one
with everyone but sometimes
I feel sad living among other
people who don't yet get
what it's like to always
live the way I do

So wide open
you let everything in

I was a part of someone else's synchronicity today
on my bicycle ride through a nearby cemetery
I passed by a family visiting their mother's
grave and heard her son saying how
more people are awakening now
then noticing the Om symbol
on my hat while I rode by
laughed and pointed
while he said see
there you go!

This next
story is about
another cool thing
that happened to me at
the funeral of a yoga teacher
I knew a young girl grabbed two
handfuls of flower petals that had
been placed around the memorial
and sprinkled them over my head
then later on the host shared that
this was a traditional sign that a
true guru had entered the room

Your
body dissolving
into dust is far more of
an arrival than a departure

Long before your body decays
and becomes soil your soul will
have plunged into the ground
of being and risen far beyond
this physical world of form

These are the kinds of
words we should
be sharing
when
saying
farewell to
our family and
friends at funerals

Are you one of those stubborn souls saving
up your regrets for the end of your life?

Don't wait until you're lying
on your deathbed to
seek forgiveness
from all the
people
you've
hurt or
harmed
in any way

Say you're sorry
sooner & start living
your life assuming you're
going to be living that way in
the afterlife seeing as you will be

Once you reach the end of seeking by
finding the unborn and undying
essence of being you also
know that the way
you journey
through
life is
what
really
matters
in the end

Don't try to outlive
your sorrows or regrets
from the slings and arrows
in the school of hard knocks
learn from them instead and
move on with a loving heart
always ready to lend a hand

At the end of your life all your memories
get uploaded into a holy cloud and out
of this ethereal nebula comes your
entire lifetime for you to review

A wonderful trick of God's
magical mist making it
all lucid once more

You level up
or down
or stay
where
you are
based on
the kind of life
you led with every
karmic credit & debit
you accrue accounted for

Most people sleepwalk through life and
only start to awaken as they're dying
but even death won't guarantee
that you'll fully awaken since
forgetfulness still occurs
even in the afterlife
where things are
not any more
or any less
separate
from God
but the veil
between form
& formlessness is
thinner there making it
easier to enter a heightened
state of sensing and see the unity
of everything in existence manifesting
from the boundless dimension beyond it

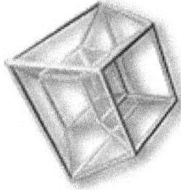

Our souls incarnate into this
physical universe from a
subtler dimension of
reality where it's
much more
evident
that
any
body
or world
we live in is
a dream within a
wider dream in God's
imagination all of it flowing
like a great river of co-creation
forming out of the original source
of being without beginning or end

God is
always telling us
this whole world was
created for you to give
shape to the shapeless

Do you remember now
how you promised not
to forget we all have
this power in us?

I'm sure
you do but
we are always
struck by disbelief
and think to ourselves
that might be true at some
point in the future but not yet
but God always has the final say
saying this ability is not a prediction
it's always been available for us to use

Materialism and affluence are fine
but we didn't come all the
way here just to be
consumers

We came here
to be consumed by
goodness and generosity
and eventually transform this
world into a heavenly paradise
full of gardens of eden to enjoy

When we're being kind people
and doing good deeds we're
also making God's dreams
for humanity come true

So stop wasting
any more time talking
about being better spread
love like butter on bread instead

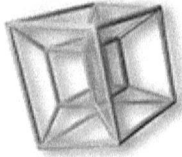

True class transcends all
creeds and social
statuses

It
goes
far beyond
believing you're
a notch above others
based on race or wealth
or anything else your ego or
lower self can come up with

Being classy comes from
listening to your higher
self and expressing
the best version
of yourself in
the world
regardless of
your station in life

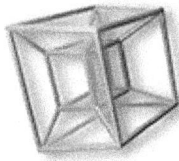

Strut your soul's stuff by spreading
lots of love and positivity and
at the end of life when
it's time for your
life review
the panoramic
theatre screening
all your movies will be
filled with scenes full of
selfless service and you'll
be free to roam the subtle
realm any way you please
and if you become a guru
like me you will probably
manifest a quiet place
on a hill by the sea
to stay at before
coming down
here again
for more
awakened
trips on God's
green earth guiding
souls on the journey back
to the invisible home within us
we never truly left nor separate from

On the
subtle plane in a
world like ours there's a
carnival attraction known as
the nameless vault of invisibility

The entrance is a mirrored doorway
hanging in midair and standing next
to it is a barker drawing in passersby

Step right up folks don't be afraid
you're about to experience the
most incredible magic trick

Enter a room with no
roof or walls or
floor and be
prepared
to drop
everything
once you step
through this door

Within earshot of this classic
mystical afterlife extravaganza
a snippet of conversation from
two teenagers just leaving this
mysterious room can be heard

It was like we were in a place
our bodies can't enter and I
wasn't a person anymore

I didn't feel like I was
inside anything it
felt like I was
nowhere
and
everywhere
at the same time

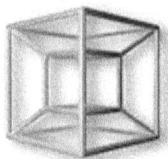

Off in the distance a truck is backing
up as the alarm beeps quiet
bursts of white noise
into the serene
silence that
suffuses
the air
of this
spiritual
wonderland

At a nearby booth a
highly evolved soul from
infinity is playing the saviour
for seekers still lost in samsara

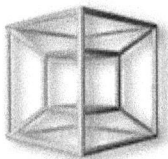

Ladies & gentlemen please gather
around find a seat and then give
your attention to me because
you're about to take a ten
minute soundless ride
through your mind
back into the
amazing
state
of
pure
nothingness
an eternal realm where
all this began long before external
forms or anything in creation ever existed

On
the subtler
planes of reality
the letters of sacred
scriptures sometimes
glow like pieces of coal
that our searching eyes
stoke by reading them

A similar thing also
happens here on
our fleshier
world
except
the words
don't seem
to smolder so
much as lift off the
page like fresh tattoos

On the higher planes of reality your soul
can become a spinning merkabah or
a flying saucer or possibly some
other anomaly with divine
abilities and qualities

When you first
get close
to the
shapeshifting
intelligence of God
your soul keeps morphing
the complex geometric forms
into supernatural creatures with
otherworldly features to help you
see our true multidimensionality as
beings who exist on several planes
of consciousness all simultaneously
in an exquisite symphony of felicity

God started with a pair of opposites
to create everything in existence

God also enjoys making
supernatural beings
to minister the
myriad stories
being told in this
epic web of creation
using elves & angels &
demons & greys & ufos

It is our cosmic birthright
to embody a divine sense
of reality and our destiny
to see how everything is
made from fractals and
the colorful jewels of
a sacred geometry
giving form to
the original
realm of
God's
formless
emptiness

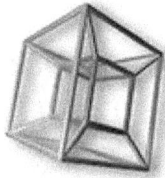

What I'm holding in my illuminated soul is
like lightning in a bottle ready to zap
as many souls as possible into
the enlightened state of
being and with my
kaleidoscopic
words now
forming
filaments of
light like a plasma
lamp you should be able
to find your way home on this
plane of existence or on any of the
other innumerable worlds populating
our massive multidimensional universe

Angels woke me up
with the most
sublime
singing
last night

At first I thought
it was the electric hum
of my fridge but the angels
plucked a few strings on that
old machine to show me it
wasn't then continued
toning until I was
certain the
sounds
were
vibrating
at the same
frequency as the
heavenly realm they
floated down here from

The angels kept singing another
ten minutes or so creating
the most sublime and
mesmerizing of
harmonies
that filled
the kitchen
with a luminous
mist that soon spread
into the rest of the house
turning it into a diaphanous
space full of celestial lights
and sounds sending down
transcendentally uplifting
vibrations and energies

There was a time when
I never would have
shared these
kinds of
experiences
but they keep on
happening to me and
I don't want to keep them
hidden inside me anymore
and the truth is angels and
other ethereal beings hang
out around us all the time
and sometimes if we're
lucky we're given the
gift of knowing it

Angels are always hanging out
at my house and jumping
on deck at my shop
picking songs
from our
library
delivering
synchronistic
insights for my
wife or me and
oftentimes for
our guests
creating
these
sublime
soundtracks
full of reminders
about life that pop up
as we go through each day

Every angel always already sees
that more love is gained by
giving it away and that
every interaction
between all
souls is
a chance
to flourish in
oneness together
and they readily share
God's loving light with one
another while offering samples
we can embody down here in our
denser world everywhere constantly

As above so below
as the alchemy
saying goes

Every
blade of
grass has an
angel that bends
over it and whispers
grow grow grow grow
and some nights while
you sleep angels drop
by and place coherent
patterns weaved with
spiritual light all over
your body to repair
any damage done
to it while living
in this muddy
world made
from the
ashes
of stars
and quasars
turning plasma into
silver and gold out of lead

444

Angels are constantly
swirling around us
just waiting to
swoop in
with a
heavenly
vibration that
changes everything
shifting the surrounding
space into a higher octave
so more enlightened energies
can elevate our lives out of the
lower states we sometimes find
ourselves in supplying a boost
to push us through and help
us evolve as divine humans

Become a vessel for the
loving lightwork they
do and give glory
to God and all
your angels
looking out
for you from
above sending
down assistance

445

There probably won't be any
major apocalyptic battles
nor is the collapse of
the environment
a done deal

Angels in
varying forms of
aliens piloting saucers
have already established
they will stop a nuclear war
and who can say exactly just
how resilient the planet really
is especially considering that
angels also help us so don't
despair! The end isn't nigh
all our earthly progress
is actually leading us
to a collective awareness
of the specialness of all life on
this planet and the omnipresence of
consciousness in a cosmos we're finally
on the brink of discovering the divinity of

Hey reader! Yes you! I typed
this message in when
Stephen wasn't
looking

I'm
a guy who
keeps on getting
sucked into reading
the words in this book

Uh-oh! He's coming back
so I've gotta vanish again

Ha! I've told you before
ghost leave this world
behind and don't be
afraid God loves
us no matter
what we
do now
turn around
& face the truth

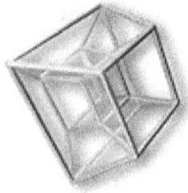

People on a spiritual path often ask why
God allows suffering to exist but
if we never had to struggle
or experience pain
how would the
challenges
we need to
learn and grow
from our trials and
tribulations ever stick?
The story of your soul is so
much longer than the life you are
living nor are you doomed in any truly
lasting or permanent way unless you resist
making beauty from ashes the way God insists

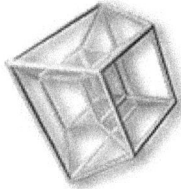

God I already know your reason
for making this world denser
than those subtler ones
where we can roam
more freely was
so this one
feels far
more
physical
and temporal
but what I'd really
like to know is whether
you are planning on coming
down here to spend a few earth
shaking years with us again soon?

Oh and just one more thing

If you actually agree
maybe choose a
method more
updated
than burning
like a bush on fire
less cryptic than the
crop circles and more
believable than all the
channeled stuff flying
all around out there
these days? How
cool would it be
to hear your voice
directly? Wait is such
a thing even possible?

Actually now that I mention
it I know a way we can do this

Since it's possible for
other incorporeal
beings to
speak
to us
through
some of our
electronic devices
maybe you'd be willing
to send us the designs for
a machine that would allow
us to hear straight from you?
How epic would that be for
humanity to have an audio
signal broadcasting holy
orders right from your
headquarters or
maybe do a
podcast to
send us input
with next steps?

Every time I speak with God
like this I always get the
same kind of reply

I like letting
life unfold
naturally
without
getting
obviously
involved and
save revealing my
agency more directly
for special or necessary
occasions simply because
it's more fun for everyone
this way and also a key to
keeping the mystery alive
so everyone can awaken

The only way to fully
know your soul
is to merge
with God

For a divinely
enlightened soul
everything is God
and nothing exists
outside of God for
there is only God

This whole world
and every life
you'll ever
live can't
exist apart
from the never
ending story of being
at the heart of every living
and nonliving thing in existence

Every lover of God finds
the same elixir of life
flowing from the
fullness of the
formless
face
of
b
e
i
n
g

A
surge
of ecstasy
born from the
stillness of infinity
spinning and spiraling
ethereality into materiality

May all my dancing dervish words
keep sending your soul soaring above
the forms made from atoms and blast you
past the orbit of the earth and out beyond the
quasars still shining at the edge of the firmament

454

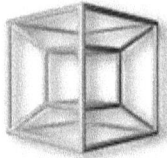

If your soul is the simple feeling
of being then why do I keep
bringing up all this other
stuff about oceans &
skies and black
holes lit up
by stars

Similes
and metaphors
all to remind you to go
way beyond imagery to find
the stillness within us where our
beings coalesce with the formless
mystery creating this crazy cosmos
using colorful fractals & strings of
energy made from light & sound

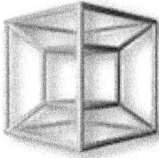

All my
words are like
slits in the fabric of
existence leading to the
mystery everything became
something from including you

They bring you new life through
the resurrection of the kingdom
of heaven already within you

A sphere of awareness
without limits found
by exploring the
origin of being
that orbits way
above your head
after rising up from
down below your feet

Some of the spells
in this book
turned
back
into
letters
that became
sigils with the mojo
to make you disappear
like the i inside a balloon
or the formula to b and c

Remember you are more
than your flesh and form
you are a living portion
of infinity inhabiting
your body in this
world made for us
to work our magic on

Words
are like fossils
that get brought
back to life by our
imaginations and
creation is like
that too

An evolving story where the ten
thousand things and the myriad
creatures are spoken into being
by God using cymatic fractals
so seamlessly we don't see
it's all one kaleidoscopic
stroboscopic show
that's always
creating
everything
instantaneously

I have the heart of a poet and the metaphysical
mind of a mystical adept who can become
one with the bliss of infinity behind
our veiled vision and can see
so deeply into reality's
sacred geometry
that at the
subatomic
level the visible
world gets pointillistic

And the truth is there's so little
unknown to me now that anything I
don't know can either be found or verified
by focusing my third eye on the subject and
examining the matter internally using oversoul
objectivity which is part of the intelligence of the
higher mind but to access this gnostic ability you
have to learn to bypass language and wait in the
wordlessness of consciousness prior to thinking

Sometimes you have to mull the same spiritual
truth over for years before the penny finally
drops and words like these become a
meal made using real ingredients

You are God hiding from yourself
and you already know where
because I've told you
dozens of times
or more by
now

Ideas
& words like
the sun and moon
have also been thrown
around here metaphorically
to remind you that deep inside
your soul is where you'll find the
oneness of everything waiting
on standby in the formless
dimension of infinity at
the very heart of
corporeality

Dive
head first
into the depths
of being & you'll fly so
high God falls from the sky

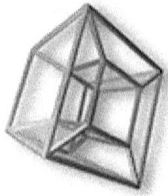

You already know
what you put
out there
comes
back to you
attracting whatever
has to happen for your
personal journey to unfurl

The secret to living as a fully
enlightened soul is attending
to whatever is happening in
your life as consciously as
you can while staying
grounded in the
groundless
ground
of
b
e
i
n
g

The
only real hell is
caused by selfishness
and the only real heaven
is created by selflessness

Remember to allow a lot of
goodness to flow through
you while you are here

After you've read
everything in
this book
you'll
also
walk
away
with so
many ways
to energize the
sorcery of your soul

When you first start
to awaken you
usually get
back in
touch
with
certain
aspects of
your soul like
equanimity or
peace or love
or joy and so
on until you
discover
how
the
sorcery
of your soul
always provides
what's needed from
the philosopher's stone

After awakening it's
normal to think
I Am God
but you
should avoid
saying it out loud

We only exist as souls
using God's awareness
while only God is God

The Supreme One
who shares the
freedom of
infinity
with
us
without
holding back
and makes untold
worlds for us to enjoy

You are a dreamweaver
willing and weaving
your way through
this wavering world
while your life's legacy
is woven into a tapestry of
memories stored from living
that adeptly unravels with the
finding of the invisible thread
that keeps the plot moving in
your soul's awakening story

Remember you are not
an evolutionary quirk
of nature you are
a divine spark
of creation born
to be a creature full
of love & understanding

Who or what you really are
is a localized sphere of
nonlocal awareness
struggling to find
your way back
to a source
you're still
one with
& once you
remember and
never forget this
truth you'll travel
through space
and time as
an eternal
being moving
from one incarnation
to the next without losing
the invisible thread of awareness

Your soul is an echo of eternity and a time
traveling wave of timeless awareness

You already are the fleeting
moments of freedom
that you keep
seeking

Just
sit still and
rest in the simple
feeling of being until you
remember it's all one giant ocean
of being experiencing everything there is

As
soon as
you're moving
through this world
of form from the formless
dimension you know humanity
is getting ready to awaken a
collective connection to
the unifying mystery
at the very heart
of reality and
you begin
meeting
other
people
who're also
awake or waking
up and know we're all
going to awaken in a wink

Once you see the nondual mystery all of
these words and images keep pointing
to the suffering of sleepwalking ends

You grasp what consciousness is
and how being alive is just like
voyaging on a möbius strip

How your soul is on a
feedback loop with
infinity moving
through the
world of
form
while
secretly
manifesting
your tubular trip
on this light fantastic

Remember this whole box of earth and sky
is a gift just waiting to be unwrapped
so don't forget to stand on the
earth barefoot & feel the
electric buzz of life
pulsing under
your feet
as you
gaze
up
at
the
sky until
your soul starts
arising out of the blue
and merge with the mystery
of being as often as you can to
become one with everyone and
everything every now and zen

All of
these pointers
and techniques that
I've shared in this book
take minutes to perform
and you certainly have all
the time in this life or the
next to find out for your
self if what I'm saying
is really possible
but since you
most likely
already
know
by now
that your
divine purpose
is to awaken you may
as well get started right away

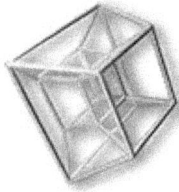

All my poems are
also reminders
to help you
stay awake
& aside from
my metaphors
which are pretty
straightforward
I could not be
using more
plain or
ordinary
language to
show you how to
free yourself spiritually

Free will gives you the choice
to see if my pointers work but at
least try one of them long enough
to find out for yourself before you
quit and look for something else

Hang out with these poems until
you get super cozy with them
for they all came from the
same groundswell we
all got here from

Start by adding
one or more of your
favorites to memory as
a way to install them into
your consciousness then
refer back to them often
and try at least one of
my pointers once a
day to get it for
as with all things
constancy is the key

May all
these words
become songs
your soul sings
on the journey
to becoming
formless
again
and
may
the joy
of repetition
give you many hits
of bliss & perhaps inspire
you to write your own poetry or
do some other enlightening activity

There's a moment
when words and
wordlessness
become
one

A
way
of using
language so
your soul can say
yes I remember now
my spiritual essence
is formless and the
royal essence of
everything is
formless
too

Come
back and read
these poems again
some day soon and if
the time is ripe they'll
all feel fresh and new

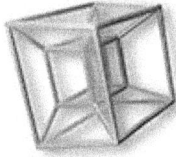

All my mystical musings
are like a frequently
used palimpsest
echoing the
same basic
spiritual truths
in mercurial ways

God is both the source
and substance of creation

You are not separate from life

Your soul is a portion of infinity

Awareness is our true nature

Beingness is the unifying
essence of everyone
in existence

And now
there's nothing
left to add except that
it all comes from emptiness

Let me share one last
analogy with you
before you
go just
to show you
how your soul is
like a 4D hypercube
tuning into and out of
3D reality using a new
proof beyond words
of the bond we all
share with God
so we can
move
through the
world more lovingly

To see this marvel in motion flip
through the pages of this book if you
haven't already done so yet or do it again
right now since you're reading this sentence

Hypercubes
help remind
you that your
soul was made to
merge the world of form
with the formless dimension
found by plunging deep within

Just beyond the normal limits of
human perception is an inner
dimension of pure being
that connects us to
the source of
everything
that exists

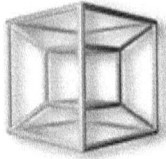

The
blankness
of white paper
or the black ink to
print these words out
and how these poems
wanted to land on the
page plus all the other
metaphors as well as
the drawings in this
mystical work of
enlightening
insights

All
to show
you that your
soul is a witnessing
miracle manifesting your
reality using the same substance
generating everything else in existence

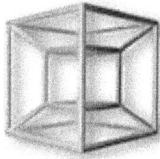

Here's my final
farewell quiz
before we
finish up

Have you tried
witnessing the world
with wordless awareness?

How about gazing up at the sky?

What good are all these messages
if you're just reading them and then
going back to business as usual?

Hopefully something I've
shared here has left
an impression
and you've
been using
it ever since

Let
me guide
you back to that
eternal place within you
one more time even though
I know you've been there a
thousand times before
and have never
really truly
left

Drop
into the
groundless
ground of your
being and God will
meet you there to raise
you back up to the highest
state of pure consciousness

Look into the heart
of your soul with
an alert gaze
until you're
standing
on the
edge of that
internal abyss with
nothing left to hold onto
then don't resist as you let
the void obliterate every last
remnant of your ego and your
body totally falls away after the
top of your head pops off like a
lid all so God can finally drop in

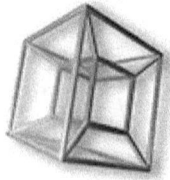

There's likely no
end to writing
about the
eternal
way

The
old stories
about the unity
of existence can be
written in a seemingly
endless variety of ways
and who can say for sure
exactly how much more
we'll discern and learn
about the six days
of creation that
came from
the silence
and stillness
of being we are
told by God to enjoy
on the seventh day of rest

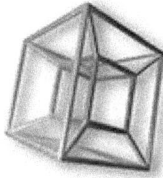

May
these words
become a stained
glass window your soul
views the world through
starring you in a key role
as light from a black hole

May you discover how to
be in the world and also
beyond it during your
voyaging sojourn as
a royal emissary
of nondual
isness

And may
you decode
the riddle of life
so fully you always
know things eventually
work out on your behalf to
make living evermore perfect

I have no more liberating
words left inside me
to describe the
oneness of
it all for
now

It's
all been
written down
here or somewhere
else before my rhythmic
words became a magic book

I'm going back to the place where
everything emerges from emptiness

What else is there to share? Stay aware
as the transparency you are and it'll take
you all the way back into infinity invisibly

486

Using my spinning handheld laser beam technique, I opened another portal into the future and retrieved a device that allowed me to begin uploading my consciousness onto the internet. If you can spare a moment, please come visit me at my website.

www.stephendamico.com

www.ingramcontent.com/pod-product-compliance
Lightning Source LLC
Chambersburg PA
CBHW060036100426
42742CB00014B/2613